B

D0267828

PRESENTING
DERMOT O'LEARY

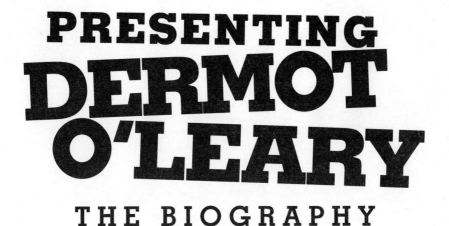

PRESENTING DERMOT O'LEARY

THE BIOGRAPHY

NEIL SIMPSON

JOHN BLAKE

Published by John Blake Publishing Ltd,
3 Bramber Court, 2 Bramber Road,
London W14 9PB, England

www.johnblakepublishing.co.uk

First published in hardback in 2010

ISBN: 978-1-84454-669-5

British Library Cataloguing-in-Publication Data:

A catalogue record for this book is available from the British Library.

Design by www.envydesign.co.uk

Printed in Great Britain by CPI William Clowes Ltd, Beccles, NR34 7TL

1 3 5 7 9 10 8 6 4 2

Papers used by John Blake Publishing are natural, recyclable products made from
wood grown in sustainable forests. The manufacturing processes conform to the
environmental regulations of the country of origin.

Every attempt has been made to contact the relevant copyright-holders, but some were
unobtainable. We would be grateful if the appropriate people could contact us.

CONTENTS

INTRODUCTION
AND THE WINNER IS

'For the judges and contestants it is time for the final result. The nation has been voting. I'm about to reveal who has won *X-Factor* 2009. Two hundred thousand people have applied and after months of fierce competition this is it.' Dermot O'Leary stood centre stage once more. Some 400 pumped-up fans were in front of him in the live studio audience. A record 13 million people were watching at home. This was Dermot's third year crowning Britain's *X-Factor* champion. It was the biggest moment on TV.

'Good luck to everyone. The winner of The X-Factor 2009 is... '

The clock shows that 23 long and painful seconds passed. On stage Joe McElderry and Ollie Murs closed their eyes and stayed close to their mentors. The X-Factor music pulsed up the tension like a heartbeat. The fans could barely breathe. Then Dermot said it.

'Joe!'

Confetti fell alongside all the tears. Cheers and applause and even some wails from Ollie's fans rang out around the studio. It was the usual moment of pure madness. But Dermot had to regain control. That was his job. It was what he excelled at.

PRESENTING DERMOT O'LEARY

'You are absolutely breathless, buddy. Congratulations, mate,' he said, his arm around Joe's shoulders, his encouragement ringing in the teenager's ears. For as Ollie, Cheryl Cole and Simon Cowell left the stage Dermot had to make sure that Joe was ready to sing that year's signature song, 'The Climb'. He had to make sure that a show that had already included performances by Sir Paul McCartney and George Michael ended on even more of a high. And it did.

Controversies would rage in the coming days as an internet campaign was launched to try and stop the *X-Factor* song from being Christmas Number One as usual. Joe's own career might not live up to all the expectations of that extraordinary night in December 2009. But as the credits rolled on the show it was clear that one man was still at the top of his game: Dermot O'Leary.

It's easy to argue that the *X-Factor* job had been something of a gamble for a man like Dermot. Yes, it had given him his biggest, prime time audience and introduced him to a whole new generation of younger fans. But right from the start it had also carried huge risks. If he had messed up then the whole country would have been watching. Perhaps more importantly, if he had done well then the whole world would have wanted a part of him. And for Dermot, surely the most private man in show-business, that would have been the biggest challenge of all.

With three series under his belt and many more to come any fears Dermot's fans may have had proved groundless. He had made the show his own. It was live television. It was the biggest show in Britain. It was his.

CHAPTER 1

HERO WORSHIP

You're eight years old. You hero-worship someone you listen to on the radio and watch on TV. And you finally get the chance to see them in the flesh. Welcome to Dermot O'Leary's world! Way back in his childhood the man he admired so much was none other than Terry Wogan. And Dermot had the chance to see him at work because back in the early 1980s one of his uncles worked as a security guard at a West London television studio. The studio where *Wogan* was filmed live, every Tuesday night.

The family connection meant Dermot saw the star-dust of TV long before most of his peers. He would have soaked up the unique atmosphere of a live studio audience. He would have seen all the bright lights hung from the iron girders on the ceilings, the huge cameras in front of the tiny set, the crowds of black-clad workers who darted around talking into what looked like James Bond style walkie talkies. Television would have been a thrilling, secret world full of cool, confident people doing vital, magical jobs. Imagine experiencing all of that at just eight-years-old. No wonder Dermot was hooked. 'From the first moment I thought, I want to do that,' he told Sunday Telegraph reporter Paul Morley years later.

Just how he might achieve his goal was another matter. For the O'Leary family, like most of us, had no other connections to the glamorous world of TV. If Dermot was to follow in Terry Wogan's footsteps he would do so through his own grit, graft and determination. And he would do so from the very unglamorous starting point of north Essex.

Colchester in Essex is proud to call itself England's oldest recorded town. It's got deep Roman roots, a castle, a zoo, a university and a military garrison. But what it certainly didn't have in the early 1970s was any form of Irish community. Most of the children born in Colchester hospitals in that decade were given the most popular names of the day. That meant there were an awful lot of very English Claires, Lisas and Julies among the girls, and a lot of boys named Michael, David and James. It also meant that Sean Dermot Finton O'Leary Junior, born in Colchester on 24 May 1973, was always going to be something of an outsider.

Dermot himself – who was always known by his second name to avoid confusion with his dad, Sean – remembers feeling like they were the only Irish Catholic family in the area. True Essex boys of that era headed to the seaside in places like Southend for their summer holidays – or went to Spain if they were very lucky and their families had a bit more cash to spend. The only holidays Dermot remembers as a boy were to his parents' native County Wexford on the south-east corner of Ireland. That's where Sean and Maria had lived before leaving for England in the 1960s – Sean with just £50 in his pocket and a lot of big dreams in his head.

They hadn't been alone in emigrating. In the 1960s hundreds of thousands of people headed east over the Irish Sea to try and escape the economic gloom in the old country. But while several other members of the O'Leary clan had also ended up in England – including Dermot's uncle at the BBC – the majority of them were still in Ireland. So there was always a very big welcome when Dermot, Nicola and their parents headed back for the summer.

The isolation of Essex was forgotten in Ireland. Over there everyone knew everyone else. They walked in and out of each other's houses and whole packs of local kids would play together in the fields, woods and streams. It was like the classic, Hollywood image of Ireland, Dermot says. But in his case it was true. Life in County Wexford was as good as his parents had always said it would be. Being Irish seemed the best thing in the whole world.

Even better was the sheer variety of life he found in Ireland – far from flat old Essex. As a boy Dermot loved being taken out to the coast for long days by the sea – though he admits he was once spooked by a pot of live crabs on Carne Pier, near Rosslare. None of them had been moving when six-year-old Dermot took a close look at them and tapped one with his finger. All were moving – and snapping their pincers – when he screamed and leapt away in terror. And the story didn't end there. His relatives still joke about how Dermot tried to hide in his uncle's VW Beetle and nearly knocked himself out by bashing his head on the door frame on the way in.

The beautiful Curracloe Beach was another favourite place for Dermot. Every spring he would count the days until he could go there again. And when he was on those famous sands he would often close his eyes and try to capture the sound of the waves crashing in the distance. Other kids put sea shells to their ears and tried to hear the sea from them. Dermot tried to hold that sound in his head, so that he could take it back to Colchester at the end of each year's holiday.

Staying connected to Ireland mattered a great deal to Dermot, so Irish influences remained just as strong when the family returned home. His dad had been a hurling champion in his youth – winning several cups and championships in southern Ireland. Sean was also a keen Gaelic football fan. And he passed that passion on to his son. The two of them would go and see games most Saturdays – and bearing in mind that they lived in the Gaelic-free zone of north Essex, this involved a fair bit of travelling. A father and son sitting in a car would naturally bond on long journeys like those. If those trips were all about an Irish sport they would also anchor you even closer to your roots. Might they distance you from the other kids who lived on your street at home? Perhaps. But as long as you had other interests and hobbies you were probably going to be OK. Most Essex boys in the seventies were obsessed by football. So was Dermot. Celtic was his first choice – his dad and most of his Irish relatives were fans and to this day Dermot says he gets a thrill when he sees that iconic green and white strip.

But after starting primary school and joining in plenty of

playground discussions about football Dermot wanted to focus on a more local team. So should he look north, to the 'tractor boys' of Ipswich Town, or south to one of the big London clubs? In 1978 the choice had been particularly stark. Ipswich had faced Arsenal in the FA Cup Final and the whole area had been obsessed with the game. For years afterwards Dermot and his school pals would discuss the match – which Ipswich won one-nil. But Dermot hadn't felt enough of a connection with the victors. He kept looking south and declared himself an Arsenal fan – not least because back then the Gunners had more than their fair share of big Irish names in its squad. The likes of Liam Brady, Frank Stapleton and David O'Leary were Dermot's early football heroes – for a long time he even told pals that David O'Leary was his uncle. 'I was the only Irish kid in town so I reckoned I could get away with it,' he jokes. But being unable to ever produce any autographs, programmes or match tickets weakened the story. So in the end he came clean and admitted that in Ireland the O'Leary name was a little bit like Smith or Jones.

Aged 11 Dermot began at his new school, St Benedict's in Colchester. And once more his love of sport helped him win some early friends. Most afternoons after school, Dermot headed out to the park with his mates for a kick-around. He tried, year after year, to get into the school team. And he gave his all in every other sport as well – from rugby and swimming to cross-country running. Written down like this it all makes Dermot sound like a classic sporty hero. In America he could have been *High School Musical*'s Troy Bolton. But in Essex, in the mid-1980s, he didn't quite attain that level of cool – because, as he happily admits today, he was always something of a nerd.

If you wanted to be in the in-crowd of a north Essex school in the 1980s, then you needed a dose of teenage angst and a full set of Smiths albums. Dermot happily admits he had neither. Yes, the first single he bought was pretty bold – 'I Can't Wait' by Portland's electro/dance band Nu Shooz. And yes, the first gig he went to was credible, though just a little predictable – it was Irish band The Pogues. But beyond that Dermot's musical tastes weren't quite as sound as they are today. He reckons the slightly offbeat The Housemartins were his favourite band, though he also had a secret love of ELO.

He also admits that when he joined mail-order firm Britannia Music Club he ticked the wrong box on the application form and was sent five CDs by the then terminally un-hip Bruce Springsteen. Dermot played them to friends in his bedroom so they could all hear just how terrible they were. The others all agreed that the CDs were only fit for the rubbish bin. But while he kept quiet about it at the time, Dermot thought differently. In 2010, his official Radio 2 biography put Bruce Springsteen in pole position among Dermot's musical favourites.

His clothes weren't quite as cool as they could be either. As teenagers, he and pal Neil Butler spent a lot of Saturdays in Colchester trying to find the right new look. But even if they found it they say it soon went wrong. A white jacket Dermot thought was the cutting edge of cool was spoiled just a little when it went in the wrong wash at home and came out an embarrassing shade of pink. And because he had no money to replace it he had to wear it for more than a year – never quite able to understand how a colour that had leached into the cloth so quickly could take so long to fade out again.

Back at school, though, Dermot was thriving – as *Hot Stars* and *OK!* magazine reporter Caroline Millington can confirm. She unearthed some old school photos of Dermot for a feature on 'stars at their schools' – and she says he looked happier and more relaxed than any of the others in her sample. 'He's one of the few people who can boast that they look half decent in their school photo. There's no mullet, goofy teeth or jug-ears in sight,' she says. Instead, Caroline simply remembers an endearingly wide smile and a cute button nose.

Dermot is happy to confirm that the smiles were totally natural. 'I know some people hate school, but I loved it,' he remembers. And his teachers loved having him. Today they say they don't want to make him feel big-headed. And they don't want to sound as if they're only praising him because he has gone on to become a star. But those that remember him say Dermot was a pleasure to teach. 'He wasn't in the top stream, academically, but he didn't disrupt lessons and he never gave any trouble,' says one of them. 'He was the kind of child you wanted in your class. He would do his homework, try hard and help out when you needed him to.'

Interestingly, Dermot's four favourite subjects as a child are mirrored in his life as an adult. They show just how grounded he is – how little his character has been changed by fame. As a 13-year-old boy he loved PE, religious education, English and drama. As a thirtysomething man he loves sport, remains a committed, practising Catholic, and reads highbrow literary fiction and non-fiction. And while he's not a great theatregoer, his day job on live television certainly brings enough drama into his life.

Back at St Benedict's the teachers also liked Dermot because he got involved. When he was older, he applied and was elected on to the school council where he helped organise charity fundraisers and put out some anti-bullying messages. One old school pal, who doesn't want to be named, says that while Dermot was on the edge of the cool kids he was never brutal about excluding those who weren't in his league. 'He wasn't one of the untouchables,' we are told. 'You could talk to him if you saw him on the bus or in the shopping centre at a weekend. I think he had felt a bit of an outsider himself when he'd been a lot younger, so he didn't make anyone else feel the same way now that he was older.'

So far, so safe. So suburban; and ever so slightly dull. Dermot is the first to admit that his childhood was almost entirely incident-free. His one key rebellion was sneaking into the Colchester Odeon aged 15, and underage, to see *Poltergeist III*. 'It wasn't worth it', he says, admitting he was more scared of being spotted breaking the rules and reported to his dad than he was of the film itself.

But as he prepared to leave St Benedict's and enrol at the new Colchester Sixth Form College Dermot was on the point of a bigger rebellion. By now he had a lot of friends in Colchester. But he was starting to wonder if the town was big enough for him. Could he settle down in a detached house on the outskirts of town, commute to London every day and raise a family in the sticks? Could he join the rat race in a bank or an office the way everyone else seemed to do? Or did he want something more?

His mum and dad certainly didn't want him to give up on education just yet. They were hoping that both Nicola and Dermot would go to university, the first in the O'Leary family to do so. But long before he filled in his application forms Dermot had two other things on his mind. He wanted to earn some money and he wanted to get a girlfriend. Pretty surprisingly, bearing in mind his current heart-throb status, he only managed to the first of the goals.

Today Dermot laughs that at school he asked the same fellow pupil out on a date a ridiculous 157 times (and he's mortified that he counted). He's more mortified still to say he got 157 rejections. 'She said years later that one more request and she would have said yes, but by then my confidence was well and truly shot,' he laughs. But he wasn't giving up. Though perhaps he should have done. He talks of another time he plucked up the courage to speak to a girl, sat down opposite her and said hello. 'She turned to her mate and stuck her fingers down her throat and made like she was being sick. So I got the message.'

When he did, finally, find someone who would be seen with him in public it still went wrong. The first girlfriend was a fellow pupil called Lindsay Turner. 'But we only dated for a week before she was robbed off me,' he told *Marie Claire* reporter Charlotte Moore, years later. He added that relationships with other girls from his classes, including Sarah Thompson and Donna Harrod, were equally short-lived. An embarrassing social failure, then? One of Dermot's school pals says he shouldn't see it that way.

'Like most schools in those days we were all talk and no action. Everything was about having a girlfriend and being seen at each other's houses, and that was all us lads talked about when we got together. But whatever we all said they were ridiculously chaste times. It wasn't quite "look but don't touch". But touch was about as far as it went and you had to be very, very lucky to get that far. Dermot might joke now that he was a bit of a loser in love. But in truth we all were,' he says.

Fortunately for Dermot he did have other issues on his mind. With romance in short supply he turned to his other new life goal. Making a bit of cash.

He and his sister had never been given much pocket money. Their parents took the view that their children would only learn the value of money if they earned it themselves. So Dermot in particular had a near endless series of part-time jobs throughout his teens. Like many Colchester kids, the first few jobs were on the land. Dermot and some friends cycled out into the Essex countryside to pick fruit, shell peas and do other farm work in their summer holidays. Back home he began washing neighbours' cars as well – and ended up winning so much work that he had to ask pals to help him out. Next up was an early-morning paper round that he kept up throughout two cold, wet winters. So by the time he reached sixteen, and had a handful of GCSEs to his name, it was little wonder he decided to find new work, indoors for a change.

His first official Saturday job was in the long forgotten

Curtis Shoes in Colchester. It wouldn't change Dermot's life. But a teenage crush on his boss certainly made it a little more interesting for a while. He earned £1.37 an hour on his Saturday shift and, as his teenage hormones raged around his body, he was head over heels in love – or certainly in lust – with the store manager. To save her from embarrassment he only refers to her as 'Mrs B'. But he has never forgotten a single detail about her. 'She was sexy, sassy and a godsend to a teenage boy. I'd have paid to be there, to be honest. She was terrific!' he jokes. So too were many of the girls who came in on a Saturday to find shoes for a big night out.

The short, polite little lad who served them tried to listen in on their conversations. He tried to find out where they might all be going and when. Could this finally be the way he could get a proper girlfriend? It's amazing to think of it today but the teenage Dermot was almost always ignored when he tried to join in these conversations. It was the same at the local swimming pool where Dermot had his next part-time job. The beautiful girls were all there at the weekends and as a lifeguard he surely ought to have been able to impress them. But somehow he wasn't. Dermot was one of Colchester Sixth Form College's good guys. He was known as a good student and a useful football player. He had plenty of money in his pockets. But he certainly wasn't setting any pulses racing. At one point in his mid-teens he seriously considered taking his religious interests to the logical conclusion and applying for the priesthood.

For all the other changes in Dermot's teenage years, one thing in his life remained constant: his top secret and on-going hero worship of Terry Wogan. As a boy he had kept on begging to go back to the west London studios to see more shows being made. And as the years passed he had many more opportunities. In 1985, when Dermot was 12, Wogan broke the broadcasting mould by being shown three times a week on BBC One. Dermot couldn't tell his school friends how excited this made him feel (they already took the mickey out of him for liking ELO and Bruce Springsteen, after all. And the pink coat hadn't exactly helped him win fashion points). But at home his family could hardly miss Dermot's mini-obsession – though they didn't entirely understand it. As often as possible every week Dermot, his mum and big sister would sit down to watch the latest show. They tuned in to see all the star guests. Dermot just wanted to watch the host do his magic. And during that very first visit to the studio, aged just eight, Dermot had done the same. After a while he had stopped being dazzled by the excitement of the new surroundings – he had begun to focus on the man in the hot seat.

Even as a boy Dermot had tried to analyse what Terry was doing. His conclusions were simple – but spot on. 'He owned the room. That's what you have to do as a presenter, to own the room,' he said years later. Dermot would try and exude that same sense of ownership up in his own bedroom in Colchester. Forget playing air guitar and faking cup-winning penalty kicks (both of which he also did). What Dermot did most was to sit in a chair, then stand up and greet imaginary guests. He looked up at the walls of his bedroom and imagined banks of seats for a live studio audience. He tried to keep one eye on all of them while interviewing the invisible figure next to him. It wasn't so much an imaginary friend, more an imaginary celebrity, he joked years later. And back downstairs three times a week Dermot watched the master so that he could perfect his art.

CHAPTER 2

THE KING OF COOL

At 14 years old Dermot was finally able to come clean to his pals about his love of TV. It was 1987 and an extraordinary new chat show had hit the screen. Being a presenter was finally about to become very, very cool.

The show was *The Last Resort* on Channel 4. The presenter was Jonathan Ross. And Dermot had a new role model – this time one who was young, cool and utterly credible. *The Last Resort*, produced by Jonathan's own Channel X company with old pal Alan Marke, was a trailblazer – at least in the UK. The show had been designed to emulate the likes of *Late Night With David Letterman* in America. The whole format was built squarely around the personality of its host. Jonathan, defying the current casual fashion trends by wearing the sharpest of suits and the boldest of ties, was a broadcasting dynamo. Dermot watched him. He loved everything about the show – a manic mix of chat, humour, interviews, music and oddities. But then there was something else. Dermot especially loved that Jonathan unashamedly broke broadcasting convention by drawing viewers in on the joke that was TV.

On *The Last Resort* Jonathan didn't try and hide the fact that he used cue cards – he threw them around the office and berated his production team if he didn't like them. And he made life behind the cameras look just as good as life in front of them. *The Last Resort* was one of the first shows to turn the cameras around and show the reality of television. It didn't try to hide the fact that it was all artifice and illusion – that the huge-looking and sexy set was just a small plywood construction in the corner of a generic, ugly studio. That kind of reality television was all new in the mid-1980s. And Dermot was hooked on it. Having been inside a traditional television studio himself he felt he was somehow closer to the action than the average viewer. He knew what they might see when the camera panned up and around. They would reveal the magic world that had mesmerised Dermot for the past six years. If watching *Wogan* had been Dermot's dirty little secret, then *The Last Resort* became his public passion. He loved going to school on a Monday so he could talk endlessly about the weekend's show. And about its host.

'Like 99 per cent of other blokes in Britain back then, I thought Jonathan was the last word in cool. Jonathan Ross was my God amongst men,' he said. Dermot also drew inspiration from the fact that Jonathan had broken through the accent barrier. 'If a man with a rough, north-east London voice can make it, when he can't even pronounce his own surname, then so, maybe, can an Irish boy from Essex,' Dermot said hopefully.

And things kept getting better. When Jonathan was pictured on the cover of style bible *The Face* Dermot was beside himself with excitement, envy – and a sudden burst of insecurity. It had seemed tough enough when he had been a lone voice wanting to follow in the footsteps of the terminally un-cool Terry Wogan. Now that everyone in the world wanted to be the new Jonathan Ross wouldn't that journey be even harder for Dermot to navigate?

'What do you want to be when you grow up?' We've all been asked that question a thousand times – so it's unlikely Dermot was any different. Most of us have sometimes given a few outrageous replies to wind up our parents – and Dermot probably did that as well. But what did he want to do? How did he reply?

'I want to become a boxer,' he had said at eighteen. The likes of the Finnegan brothers, Paddy Maguire and Pat McCormack were boxing legends in the Irish community back then. But the O'Learys didn't really want their son following in their footsteps. So with that out of the way Dermot moved on. A professional diver was next on his list, though looking back he says he has absolutely no idea why. Then, having worked briefly as a waiter at Colchester's Bistro Nine restaurant, he said he was considering training as a chef – many years before the likes of Gordon Ramsay came along and proved this could be a very lucrative career option.

What Dermot should have done was tell his parents the truth: that nearly a decade after being led into his first television studio he still believed that this was the place he should work. Whether this could be anything more than a pipe-dream was another matter, however. Most Irish dads wanted their kids to get what they would probably call 'a proper job'. They would like their sons to follow traditional, firmly masculine career patterns and to keep their feet firmly on the ground. They would also try to instil simple values into their children. Work hard, play by the rules, do the right thing. Aspirations and ambition were good. But dreams were only for dreamers. Education was also important to most families in north Essex in the seventies. Parents who had never been to university themselves hoped their kids would have the opportunities they had missed.

Going to university did something else for the children of aspirational parents. It bought them time. Time to work out what they really wanted to do. Time to consider a whole range of jobs, careers and professions. Time to make friends as well as mistakes. If you ended up at the right college, in the right company, then you could bypass the recession and leapfrog into the job of your dreams. Well, that was the theory.

The roll call of famous alumni from Middlesex University in north London suggests the place was some sort of 'kids from Fame' stage school. Helen Mirren, Vic Reeves, Johnny Vegas, Alan Carr, Adam Ant, Alison Goldfrapp and fashion designer Vivienne Westwood have all passed through its doors. But when Dermot arrived – just as the university upgraded itself from its old Polytechnic status – the intake was a little less starry.

In the early 1990s, the university was going against national trends by recruiting an above-average percentage of mature and overseas students. It added up to a uniquely diverse student body. But Dermot didn't feel entirely at home there.

He was as sporty as ever. He joined a loosely organised football league while spending a lot more time on his favourite sport: rugby. In his final year he was on the verge of winning a place in the university's first team, though an excess of talented players meant he never quite made the cut. He got a little political, the way most students do, following up his time on his old school council by attending plenty of student council meetings and briefly considering standing for election to it. He embraced campaigns against third world debt, and has kept that passion alive until this day.

But while Dermot did make a firm set of close friends he didn't always get the student mentality. 'I met more morons at university than anywhere else in my life,' he says. And this from a man who made a career alongside *Big Brother* housemates and interviewed George Galloway, Michael Barrymore and Pete Burns.

Two issues left Dermot cold at Middlesex. First, as a typical Gemini, he reckons he gets bored very quickly. He felt in too much of a hurry for a three-year course. He didn't see how one subject could be worthy of that much study. The next issue was the course itself. Dermot had decided to do a degree in Media and Television Studies with a minor in Politics. He happily admits he was being cynical and single-minded when he chose it. He examined prospectus after prospectus from universities, colleges and polytechnics around the country and felt the Middlesex offering would be most likely to help him break into the broadcasting industry.

Looking back he accepts that his expectations were far too high.

Academia was just that – a little too academic and not quite practical enough for his needs. A lot of the time he didn't see the point of his lessons or his lectures. He was focused solely on learning enough to force his way into a television studio. His tutors seemed focused solely on explaining the intricacies of post-war German cinema and the new wave of film-makers in Scandinavia. And all the while Dermot worried that he had made a mistake by opting out of the workplace for three years while he completed his degree.

The early 1990s were the height of the new media studies boom. Many critics still wrote the subject off as a Mickey Mouse degree. But to someone like Dermot, with no connections to tap for a way into the media world, it had seemed the only way to push at the door. 'Have I made a mistake?' he asked himself as the course work became more and more theoretical and obscure. 'Am I missing the boat by sitting in lectures when I should be getting my hands dirty at the coal face?'

What made Dermot's university career at the same time more enjoyable and more nerve-racking was the fact that less than an hour south-east of his campus a new television revolution was being played out. *The Big Breakfast* had been launched in a set of converted lock-keepers' cottages in Bow, east London. Its presenters, Chris Evans and Gaby Roslin, were doing everything that the 19-year-old Dermot had ever wanted to do. They had taken up the mantle from Jonathan Ross and made live television even more knowing, more accessible and more manic. Throw in Paula Yates interviewing celebrities on the *Big Breakfast* bed and student life was never going to be the same again.

At Middlesex Dermot and his fellow students talked endlessly about this incredible new show. They loved to read about the fuss it was causing among its more staid breakfast rivals. Every close call over swearing or adult humour was seen as a triumph by the media students. Every missed cue or failed link was a masterclass on how to carry on regardless. But however much he loved to watch and talk about the show, Dermot felt the same insecurity that had crept up on him at 14 when Jonathan Ross first hit the screens. To Dermot's mind, being Chris Evans was clearly the most desirable job in the country. So surely everyone in the country would try and steal it from him. 'How can I compete with all of them?' he asked in his low moments – less willing than ever to throw himself into a deconstruction of classic Swedish cinema or an analysis of how Lend-Lease affected the post-war political dynamic in Westminster.

With so many worries crowding his mind, graduation couldn't come fast enough for Dermot. Yes, he enjoyed much of the sporting and the social side of his degree. He would have lapped up the all-too-rare time he got to spend in the university's mocked-up television and radio studios and editing suites. He collected a very average 2:2 BA in Media and Television Studies along with that minor in Politics.

Then he realised it was crunch time.

His new hero, Chris Evans, had just left *The Big Breakfast* and was creating even more mayhem (and making even more money) on *Don't Forget Your Toothbrush*. The success of this new show, and the endless newspaper articles about the men who were jostling to succeed Chris on *The Big Breakfast*, meant that becoming a television presenter was now the key goal for a whole generation of young people.

So how could Dermot stand out from the crowd?

The one skill he knew he had was the ability to talk to anyone about anything – and hopefully to charm them. He reckons that the gift of the gab is the gift of the Irish. He had been born with it – and he had honed the skill by learning from another master: his dad Sean. 'My dad is the biggest schmoozer on earth; he can talk the hind legs off a donkey,' Dermot laughs. That same skill had come in useful at university when Dermot had first arrived at Middlesex and wanted to make friends. He hoped the skill wouldn't desert him now he was entering even more uncharted waters.

As he headed back to Essex to stay with his parents while he looked for work, Dermot at least knew he didn't have to worry about money. Having had part-time jobs since the age of 11, he had always had cash in his pocket. He hadn't had a full grant at university, but his parents had always helped out when he had needed them. And he had carried on with a host of part-time jobs in his holidays and during some term times. So in 1995 he was prepared to play a long game. He knew he would probably have to work for low or no wages when he started working in media. But he knew too that the experience he could gain – to say nothing of the contacts – could be priceless. But where would be start?

Sitting in his old bedroom in north Essex Dermot knew his

options were relatively limited. Essex didn't have any local television stations. Many people in the south tuned in to the LWT and the BBC's London stations. Others chose the East Anglian alternatives which were broadcast from Norwich. And as far as Dermot was concerned Norwich might as well have been the moon. If he did make it on screen he certainly didn't want to spend his time talking about farm crime and fertilizer, which was all he ever seemed to see covered on *Look East*. Nor did he feel that Anglia's one truly national television show, *Sale of the Century*, 'Live from Norwich', suited his personality.

So Dermot looked south to Chelmsford. He would try and get into television by taking a circuitous route. He applied for unpaid work experience on BBC Radio Essex. If he got it, then he could feel he was finally on his way.

CHAPTER 3

RADIO DAYS

In the mid-1990s local radio stations were a very strange place to be. Many were rightly derided as the home of very real 'Smashie and Nicey' types, the dreadful, hammy old has-been DJs derided in the infamous *Harry Enfield's Television Programme* sketches and played by Harry Enfield and Paul Whitehouse. Those sketches are said to have triggered the end of several long careers at Radio One, including those of Simon Bates and Dave Lee Travis. Local radio DJs were seen by some as no better than hospital radio amateurs, the broadcasting equivalent of embarrassing uncles dancing at weddings, spinning discs and making everyone cringe.

But for all this mockery there was something else. Yes, everyone seemed to laugh at local radio presenters, but in some ways it was all a front. Deep down all the critics would have jumped at the chance of changing places with the people they professed to despise. Local radio might be a joke. But being a local radio DJ was still seriously desirable. And that was especially true in Essex. Because Essex was different.

The county had always been central to the whole pirate radio era that hit a peak in the 1960s and has kept afloat ever since. Many of the most famous pirate radio ships had broadcast from just off the Essex coast, so while their signals went national their influence was most keenly felt in the local area. Police action against them was always big news. The DJs were outlaw heroes. For a while it seemed like everyone in 1980s Essex felt a sneaking admiration for the wildest of the DJs. Their patter was a long way from Terry Wogan's cosy, mainstream chat. But they were still entertainers. They were also the future.

In 1981, the same year that eight-year-old Dermot was being taken to Shepherd's Bush to see *Wogan*, Essex got its first commercial radio station. Essex Radio broadcast out of studios in the county town of Chelmsford and was a hit from the start. Little wonder the BBC decided the Essex airwaves were far from saturated. In 1986 BBC Radio Essex was launched, with a bang, on bonfire night. And Smashie and Nicey were nowhere to be heard.

From day one, BBC Radio Essex was designed to be different. It had too much competition from the pirates, from London's Capital Radio and, of course, from Essex Radio, for it to toe the BBC line and do the whole public service, local information thing. Worthy but dull wouldn't work in Essex. That's one reason why the station was the only one in the BBC family not to have the corporation's insignia included in its official logo. Instead, BBC Radio Essex had to be cool. The managers deliberately sought younger, hipper DJs, presenters and newscasters. They wanted a red-top, tabloid style for the news and a celebrity-focused *Hello!* magazine style for the music shows.

The idea was a trailblazer – a commercial gamble that was successful years ahead of its time. So forget the dinosaurs on Radio One and the fossils on Radio Two. Forget the amateurs on local stations around the country. The DJs in Essex were the epitome of cool. Listeners had always been able to tell how much fun the presenters were having on their shows. They were laughing as much as everyone's heroes on television. And they were everywhere. The station did roadshows and outside broadcasts. The staff were the new celebrities of the country. And everyone wanted to join them on the air.

Andrea Hughes, who worked in the BBC Radio Essex head office in Chelmsford in the late 1980s and early 1990s, remembers how intense the competition became for work. 'They were absolutely crazy times and getting on to a local radio station in those years was one of the toughest things you could do. It's hard to imagine just how many letters – desperate letters – we were sent every day. Then there were the people who turned up at our studios every day, desperate to get interviews and ready to work for nothing if that was what it took. They would leave tapes they had made of themselves hosting made-up shows at home. Or they would leave presents for the DJs with the tapes inside them – hollowed out boxes of chocolates were particularly popular for a while, and we got a lot of tapes, CVs and letters with tea bags stapled to them so they could be read while we had a cup of tea. Kids of all ages, from primary school up, were obsessed by radio back then. They saw us as the coolest job they could ever do. But hardly any of them ever made it. Because there was so much demand, almost all the requests for work experience or jobs were rejected – they had to be.'

But Dermot got in. We can't know what it was about his approach that worked – we can't even be sure if there were any tea bags attached to his initial letter! What we do know is that he made it in where so many others failed. So many people were desperate for the station's ultimate prize: work experience with the chance to go on the air if they made the grade. So many people had interviews, informal chats and voice tests. So many of them fell by the wayside. Dermot didn't. He made it.

The Chelmsford-based producers who worked alongside him in his first few months remember him as a breath of fresh air. 'He was nervous, you could tell that. But he was confident as well,' says one. 'One other word defines him: fresh. He was bright and breezy and like most kids of his age he had limitless energy and enthusiasm. With hindsight it is always easy to say you could see some extra spark in people who go on to become big successes. But even if we didn't all spot it at the time it was clear that Dermot was the kind of person who would make the most out of every opportunity that came his way.'

For many months, though, the key opportunities that came Dermot's way were prosaic, to say the least. As the new work experience boy he wouldn't be trusted with a microphone for some time. Instead he simply helped out in the studios. He made and brought in the tea. He went out to buy newspapers and magazines before all the topical shows and phone-ins began. He booked taxis for the DJs so they could get to their well-paid personal appearances after their shows. He paid his dues.

His voice nearly made it on to the air after he was given his first real challenge on the station: to head out on to the streets of Chelmsford with a microphone to record shoppers' thoughts about the day's news. Sometimes he forgot that he wasn't supposed to prompt his subjects or interrupt their flow with thoughts of his own. Sometimes he did it so often it seemed as if his contributions would have to be broadcast along with those of the station's listeners. But in the end the editors always found enough clean content. And still Dermot waited to take to the airwaves.

As he did so Dermot kept dreaming about how his own show might sound. He reckoned his musical taste had improved hugely since his teens, and he was sure he could put together a killer playlist. And he was sure he could make people laugh as well. He remembered all the long, funny stories on Terry Wogan's Radio Two show. He remembered how his mum had almost cried with laughter listening to them some mornings. He was convinced he could spin the same kind of tales.

But would he get the chance?

Work experience stints always pass too fast. The days or weeks rush by in a flurry of new faces and new challenges. The sheer excitement of walking into the building you've dreamed about can be intoxicating. As you step in off the street you can allow yourself to believe that everyone's looking at you, that they're watching jealously as you greet the receptionist and disappear towards the studios. Anyone who saw Dermot walk in to Radio Essex might have tried desperately to work out who he was. They might have looked at him and thought: he's made it, he's arrived. But in reality he hadn't. And for all the fun and the vox pops a great deal of all work experience stints involve the dull, day to day events that could just as well have taken place inside a provincial solicitor's office. It would have been quite wrong for him to think that as the latest work experience boy he could go so much further than anyone else. Radio wasn't like the theatre. Dermot wouldn't be the understudy who could be plucked from the wings one night as an unknown and leave the theatre as a star.

Dermot hadn't arrived. He was eating away at his savings and his goal of being the next Terry Wogan, Jonathan Ross or Chris Evans were as far away as ever. And to make him feel even worse Chris had just launched yet another fabulously anarchic show on Channel 4.

TFI Friday had everything a budding TV presenter could have wanted. But as an outsider the drawbridge to that closed world was held up as tightly as ever. 'How do I break my way in?' That was the only question media studies students ever really want to ask. 'Dissecting the symbolism of post-war German cinema is all very well. But how the hell can I get a job in a studio?' they want to scream at their tutors week in and week out. Dermot had very probably wanted to ask these same questions – with a little more finesse – of all his radio colleagues back in Essex. But it would have been a little tricky. Some radio presenters have a chip on their shoulders when it comes to TV. They hate the perception that they are second-class citizens in the broadcasting world. They certainly don't take kindly to people who are simply using radio as a stepping stone to 'better' things. The most diplomatic thing for someone like Dermot would have been to ask them how he could get full-time, paid work on that or any other station. The answer would surely be pretty much the same for television. So what could that answer have been? 'Write in, ring up, keep trying and hope you get lucky. Someone has to,' pretty much summed it up.

So off Dermot went.

Back in his room in Colchester he found a copy of *The Broadcast Directory* and went to work. He wrote down an endless series of names and addresses and sent his CV to anyone and everyone he thought might have a job to hand out. It was a long list. In all Dermot reckons he wrote more than 200 letters. Television stations, production companies, individual shows, agents and anyone else connected to the business all got letters from people like Dermot every day. Next to none of them even bothered to send a reply. Every week he also scoured the media sections in the newspapers, and the new trade titles he had on subscription. It didn't matter what jobs were being advertised there. If the advert included the word 'television' in almost any context then it might be worth sending in an application.

'The trouble with the television industry is that getting in is part of one of those cosmic catch-22 situations. You can't get in unless you've got experience, and you can't get experience until you've got in,' says freelance reality television producer Cathy O'Neill. 'You need to be incredibly determined, persistent, thick-skinned and ultimately lucky to break the circle. You have to think laterally. What you mustn't do is give up.'

Dermot didn't – though a lot of the time he came very close.

Day after day he must have sat in Colchester waiting to see if the post man would bring anything – and job applicants always say that even a standard issue rejection on production company headed note paper was better than nothing. At least that meant their applications had actually arrived, even if it hadn't necessarily been read. At least it proves that something is going right.

But after a while the strain starts to tell when you feel you're constantly bashing against a brick wall. Should you give up and get 'a proper job' after all? Should you follow some other road instead? Just how long do you wait for a dream that might never quite come true?

We now know for certain that Dermot didn't give up. He may, though, have come close to running out of money. Job-hunting can be an expensive business – and it's not a lot of fun. Dermot was still busily applying for jobs at 23. That was when he got the letter.

A documentary production company based out in far-from-glamorous Hammersmith was offering a new opportunity as a 'runner' – the classic way into the television industry. Dermot slept on a friend's floor in south London the night before his interview and was so terrified of being late for the appointment that he arrived nearly a full hour early. The nerves that his Radio Essex colleagues had seen were very much on display in the hour-long interview. But so too was that freshness.

Something clicked and he was offered the job. Dermot O'Leary was in the television industry at last. His foot was in television's door and he was so thrilled he could barely breathe – just like when he'd been a boy on the way to his first-ever *Wogan* show.

He remembers his first day at the company passing in an excited blur. He remembers his first few weeks passing with just as much optimism and excitement. But then a few doubts started to creep in.

Dermot looks back at the company's staff with affection and has never spoken less than highly of his time there. But was the firm a proper fit for his personality? His new employer was yet to make the popular, often pop-based shows it created from the end of the nineties onwards. In Dermot's day it specialised in less eye-catching medical, current events and historical productions. Not everyone would have been excited by the firm's output back then. Nor by its location out in Hammersmith. The company wasn't based in the BBC's Television Centre or the LWT Tower and it wasn't producing *The Last Resort*, *The Big Breakfast* or *TFI Friday*. A lot of Dermot's contemporaries back in Essex may never have watched any of the shows the company made. But at least it made shows. At least it was television. It was a start.

But Dermot knew that if his break into TV was a marathon then he had barely made it past the starting line. It was also very clear that he was at the bottom of the food chain in his new role. In some ways it was just like work experience in radio. The only difference was the wages. On work experience you get no money. As a television runner you get next to no money.

'When you're a runner you're pretty much the lowest of the low,' says reality television producer Cathy O'Neill. 'It's the kind of role that pretty much wouldn't be allowed in any other industry because it's so menial. And the most extraordinary thing about it is that in television it's done by hugely qualified people. You can have a PhD or a master's degree and still spend all day photocopying scripts. And you do it because you never know whether one day you might be at that damn photocopier at just the right time. You might overhear the producers talking about a vacancy that you would be perfect for. That can be the moment you get in ahead of all the other wannabes.'

So that's what Dermot did. He made the tea at Barraclough Carey Productions, just as he had done back in Essex. He went out to buy people their lunches, he collected dry cleaning and he loitered by that photocopier. In short, he paid his dues once more. He also listened, watched and learned. Independent production companies didn't have in-house studios. They tended to rent other studios when their projects got to the production stage. Dermot was always first to volunteer to help when the team headed to them. He wanted to see first-hand how a proper studio worked. He wanted to make contacts and get his face and name known. And he loved it. In the studios he could forget that some of the work he did was dull. He could be forgiven if once or twice he had imagined walking into the studio to film his own show. He might have imagined a warm-up artist calling out: 'Ladies and Gentlemen, it's Dermot O'Leary!' as he stepped onto the set. But would those words ever be used for real?

When you are 24 years old and in your first full-time job, then a year can feel like for ever. It certainly did for Dermot.

He didn't have enough cash to 'celebrate' his first anniversary as a runner. Every month seemed to last a lot longer than his wage packets and he spent too much time in grotty flat-shares and even sleeping on friends' floors for a few weeks at a time to save cash.

The glamorous world of television had certainly passed him by. But still he stuck at it.

One year became 18 months and still he made the teas, collected the lunches and hailed the cabs. The good news was that away from the office he had made plenty of new friends – or at least he hoped he had. It's a sad fact that most newcomers to television feel that a small part of them is always on edge, always looking over their shoulders. Every day new workers worry that someone else might have slipped ahead of them. And in truth they're not being paranoid. The evidence suggests that often in television, everyone really is out to get you. 'The problem with this industry is that despite all the camaraderie, all the late nights out boozing, all the coupling up and copping off among staff you are always, always aware that you are all in competition with each other for the next job,' says one former television runner who doesn't want to give her name. 'You're always doubting and questioning yourself. Am I young enough, cool enough, cute enough? Do I make enough jokes, do I laugh at enough jokes? Do I like the things that my bosses like, am in the in-crowd in this team or am I the one they wouldn't pick for a game of softball at the summer picnic? You need to develop a very thick skin – and a very good bullshit detector.'

Cathy O'Neill says there was also something else. Something equally cynical but absolutely true. 'Some very nasty, unpleasant people do get to the top in television. But in general it really doesn't pay to make enemies, especially when you are starting out. A better strategy is to be nice to absolutely everyone. Someone you might have dismissed as going nowhere the week before might suddenly be promoted into a recruitment role today. So the last thing you ever want them to know is that you always thought they were a loser. If you want to get from a runner's role to something better, you need to be "always on" and you need to be everyone's friend, all of the time. If you get a reputation for dragging people down then you might as well give up your dreams. Television needs "up" people who can lift a mood and see a team through the stresses and strains of a big production.'

If he did nothing else at Barraclough Carey, Dermot certainly did that.

His gift of the gab seemed to carry him through all the office politics and any production crises. He might have a soft north Essex accent, but he was a true Irish charmer. People genuinely liked him – not least because he was always ready to laugh at himself. Former colleagues from that era – when the offices were shared with staff from several other major production firms – say that he always told loads of jokes, mostly at his own expense. One story that always got laughs – and some nice sympathy from women – was the one about the time he was struck by lightning when he was just five years old. 'Did it hurt? Were you OK? Did you need to go to hospital?' he would be asked.

Then he always came clean. 'I didn't actually get hit at all, I just saw some lightning in the distance when I was a little boy and because it looked so cool I made myself believe I had been hit by it,' he admitted. He also told jokes about all the times at school when he had tied himself up in knots trying to persuade his pals that Arsenal star David O'Leary was indeed his uncle.

How long can you keep on laughing when you're worse off than you were as a teenager and convinced you've left it too late to get the job of your dreams? In their bleaker moments every lowly television runner probably asks themselves those questions. Should they stay where they are for 18 months? Two years? The rest of their working lives? Or should they just give up altogether?

Most young people are lucky enough to have parents who can help snap them out of their self-pity. When they go home for the weekend they're not allowed to moan. They're reminded that as far as most people in their home towns are concerned, they are already a success. For Dermot this kind of message would have been even easier to get across. After all, he really had followed his dreams and was working in the industry he had always loved. And he was putting down firm foundations for the future. His job might be menial and badly paid but it certainly gave him a proper grounding in his chosen profession. Years later, when he became one of our most recognised stars, Dermot acknowledged the debt he owed his time at Barraclough Carey. 'Getting experience behind the cameras was a great start. Being a runner taught me how television is made and how all the different parts of a production come together. I would have struggled to do well in front of the cameras if I hadn't found out what was going on over on the other side.'

PRESENTING DERMOT O'LEARY

And after a little more than 18 months on that toughest of apprenticeships Dermot was finally heading out of Hammersmith and into the heart of things. He had been making contacts, shaking hands, kissing cheeks, applying for jobs and trying to get a next step up the career ladder throughout his time as a runner. Suddenly it seemed to have paid off. He was offered a new job. And this time it looked to be a perfect fit for his personality.

CHAPTER 4

THE WARM-UP
MAN

Channel 4 was Dermot's spiritual home. It was where all the coolest young stars worked. It broadcast all the most cutting-edge programmes. And it had plenty of money to spend. Getting a job on the channel had been his goal for more than a decade when he finally walked though its Charlotte Street headquarters and went to the human resources office to complete his application process.

Trouble was, in some ways Dermot's new job wasn't much of an improvement on his old one. He was a researcher. In the food chain of television it did rank a lot higher than a runner. But it was never going to be an easy ride. And the learning curve would often be eye-wateringly steep. 'It is the hardest job on telly,' Dermot says of television research. 'It's like telesales. You're on the phone all day. It's back-breaking and demoralising. It's not glamorous at all. It's harder than producing. It's certainly harder than presenting. You get all these CVs from people wanting to be researchers and I'm sure that half of them can't know what it involves.'

For Dermot the job involved some very long hours and some very stressful days. After shadowing his new colleagues for a couple of weeks, the first big show he worked on was called *Century Road*. The idea was to tell the story of a 100-year-old street through the memories of its oldest residents. Dermot's role was to nail down a skeleton story of that history, then to find the residents who could bring it to life. And from the very start he felt as if fate was on his side. The street the production team had chosen was in Jonathan Ross's old neighbourhood of Walthamstow, north-east London. How different life – and television – might have been if Dermot had actually met him back then!

With a rough idea of the story he wanted to tell, Dermot then headed out of the office. He arrived in Walthamstow and started knocking on doors to get stories and interviews. His aim, on that first day out in the field, was to get enough good content to really impress his new bosses. He failed.

The rebuffs and the refusals began early and didn't let up. Most doors on Century Road, London E17 were never opened. Those that were didn't provide the information, or the characters, that Dermot required. 'Sorry mate, I'm new here myself,' was a constant refrain. 'Mummy and daddy are out,' became another one. Then came the biggest frustration of all – Dermot finally found what he was looking for. She was an elderly lady who knew all about the street's history. She had been living in the same house almost all her life. She had survived the Second World War on the street and looked set to be an absolute goldmine of information. Except for one small thing. She didn't want to talk. 'She wanted nothing to do with me,' Dermot says with a smile. She was polite, but firm, in a way only old ladies can be. But she bid him on his way and closed the door.

Dermot did not give up and walk away. He carried on working. But it wasn't always easy. There were more unanswered doors, more recent arrivals, more latchkey kids waiting for their parents to come home. And very little street left to research.

'Hello there, it's me again, from the television company.' After a couple of fruitless days Dermot was back at his old lady's door. Still she didn't want to talk. So the next day he started to bring her gifts – flowers at first, then chocolates when he thought she might finally be coming around. But would the charm offensive work?

'She was still like, "Get away from me!" And I was a bit worried I might get in trouble for bothering her,' he says. But in the end he won the day. This most important of ladies did ultimately succumb to the O'Leary charm. She recorded her memories on camera, gave him the names of a few other former neighbours who could add anecdotes of their own, and helped Dermot score valuable brownie points back at the office.

Exhausted but euphoric, Dermot sat in the editing suite when the show was being put together. Strictly speaking that wasn't part of his job. But as usual he wanted to watch and learn about every aspect of the television industry. And he wanted to make sure his little old lady's best bits didn't end up on the cutting room floor.

After *Century Road* Dermot moved on to an ever-changing roster of other shows. Sometimes he just helped out for a few weeks, sometimes he was tied to a project for an entire series.

And sometimes he felt that for every step he took forwards he might also be taking one back. Researcher roles on Channel 4's quiz, chat and discussion shows tended to involve identifying potential guests, tracking them down, sounding them out and checking whether they were available to be part of the programme in question. Then there was all the dull stuff. Arranging their transport, lowering their expectations of any fees, greeting them on the day and being on hand before, during and after the recording in case there was anything they needed. This is where the worries can easily seep in for the lowly staff members. Once again they can find themselves buying lunches, making coffees and standing out in the street looking for cabs – just the way they might have done in all their previous jobs.

It's easy to feel that you're getting nowhere.

It would be equally easy to give up – or to get angry about it.

As far as we know, Dermot did neither. He carried on working hard. And in the end he got his reward.

Everything changed for Dermot when he started arranging the guests for *Light Lunch* in 1997. The new Channel 4 chat and comment show was easily the biggest and most high-profile production that Dermot had ever worked on. And he loved it from the very start. Comediennes Mel Giedroyc and Sue Perkins were the show's presenters and they laughed their way through their lunchtime slots – attracting tens of thousands of new viewers in the process.

As far as Dermot was concerned the show's studio location was one of the best things about it. It was broadcast from The

London Studios, the new name for the old LWT Tower on Upper Ground on the South Bank of the River Thames in London. That iconic tower has been home to every television legend from Bruce Forsyth and Les Dawson to Dame Edna Everage and Cilla Black. It was the home of the star-studded *An Audience With* extravaganzas, and it ranked alongside the BBC in west London as the heart of the entertainment establishment. With one main stage and a set of flexible, smaller studios it was constantly humming with activity. Just walking through the warren of corridors gave Dermot a thrill. Larger-than-life-sized portraits of past and present ITV stars lined the walls and you never knew when one of these people might be on the other side of the lift doors as they were whisked up to the stars' dressing rooms on the first floor or the glorious hospitality suite on the eighteenth near the top of the tower.

Dermot must surely have smiled as he was waved past security every day. Trouble was, he wanted more than just a researcher's or a runner's job. He wanted real involvement on the studio floor. And by chance he was about to get it.

Like most live television shows, Mel and Sue's producers didn't want the cameras to roll when the studio audience was cold. All shows need atmosphere and there is only a select band of people who can provide it. 'The industry has a small number of totally reliable warm-up staff. They're great at making an audience relax and getting them laughing. They spell out the ground rules – saying when everyone needs to applaud and make some noise and when they need to shut up. They make people feel part of the show and not intimidated by the surroundings. You're really a cross between a stand-up comedian and a flight attendant which is a tougher role than it sounds. And it is vitally important to get it right,' says Channel 4 producer Martin Reynolds.

Today, people like Andy Collins on *The Paul O' Grady Show* are recognised as warm-up royalty. And their patter is genuinely funny. 'Ladies and gentlemen, before we start this evening I'm legally required to tell you all about the emergency exits in the studio. As you'll see by the signs the nearest exits are behind me, here, and at the back of the studio over there. But, really, there's no need to be alarmed. It's extremely unlikely that this studio will have a dangerous fire. Again...' is one of the industry's favourite lines.

But when Dermot arrived on the scene at *Light Lunch* even this kind of comment wasn't raising much of a laugh. The warm-up man was leaving the crowd stone cold. So in typically brutal television fashion he was fired. The producers needed to find a new fast-talker overnight. And they chose Dermot.

In almost every way it was a gamble – for all sides. Dermot didn't exactly have any experience as a stand-up comedian or performer. But no one seemed to care. Everyone seemed to think that after the last guy Dermot could hardly be worse. Unfortunately, everyone was wrong.

The following day Dermot's first audience wasn't just left cold, it was locked in some kind of permafrost. He had been like a terrified best man at a posh, high-society wedding. His voice was weak, his delivery poor and his jokes totally inappropriate to the occasion. Nothing he said worked. And having seen his first few 'funny' lines fall flat he wasn't able to recover. 'Television audiences are like sharks. They can smell fear. If you're first few lines fail you reek,' says comedian Lloyd Pierce. Dermot reeked and was mortified. 'My first show was just awful. Afterwards I sent out a circular to the production team saying that I was going to throw myself off Hungerford Bridge if anyone wanted to come and watch, because it would be funnier than my warm-up,' he remembers with a rueful smile – the only one he raised that entire day.

But the producers gave him another chance the next day, not least because they didn't have anyone lined up to take his place at such short notice. And on day two a few members of the lunchtime audience did crack a few smiles. On day three there were some laughs. And by the start of his second week Dermot had finally found his stride. People on the show say that the transformation came when Dermot decided to be himself.

'At first, like a lot of warm-up people who are nervous about their material, he tried to copy some of the other big comedians of the day,' says one of the team. 'Back then everything was about being jaded and cynical and political but that should never have been Dermot's style. The audience could tell they were being short-changed by someone whose heart wasn't in it. It felt as if they were getting a Ben Elton-lite. It was only when Dermot dropped all that and bounced around the front of the crowd, mike in hand, with a big smile on his face and an open admission that he was terrified that the crowds got it. It was only when he talked about his journey to the studio, his chronic forgetfulness and his other failings that they started to laugh. He was as self-deprecating then as he is now. He always began with jokes at his own expense and he was great with people in the audience. He was warm and likeable. He was a bit of a clown. He jollied people along and set the tone for the show. We loved him.'

The producers gave the transformed Dermot a longer-term commitment to the show. It didn't get him in front of the cameras. But it was a big step up from his days as a lowly runner. And it could have been the first step of many. A few key people in the *Light Lunch* offices were starting to wonder if their new warm-up man could be a hot property in his own right. He didn't know it at the time, but Dermot was being watched like a hawk. His bosses were wondering just how far this happy young character could go.

After finishing his first full month in the warm-up role, Dermot reckoned he had learned three key lessons. The first was that it never paid to try and be someone you aren't. The second was that he loved having a microphone in his hand. The third was that he thrived on the freedom to pace around the studio in search of laughs. Not for Dermot was the newsreader style of sitting safe behind a big wide desk. His warm-ups involved plenty of chat with the audiences, plenty of questions, comments and quick chats. Dermot loved being able to race up the metal steps of the seating sections to share a few words with someone on the edge of an aisle. He was always just as ready to squeeze along a row to get to someone in the middle of the studio who had thought they were safe from his attentions.

Looking back it's easy to see how his warm-up acts would, ultimately, set the format for almost all the other good television he would do.

'Thank you everybody and enjoy the show!' After giving what would soon be his trademark mini salute and bow, Dermot would leave the stage to head back into the wings. Mel and Sue then hosted their show with a happy, receptive audience ready to laugh at every joke and play along with every piece of fun.

Dermot got on well with both Mel and Sue. He certainly respected the tough career paths they had taken to get their own show – both having paid a lot of dues on the stand-up circuit. But he still wished he could step into their shiny shoes one day. In some ways his arrival as warm-up man had been a bit like the understudy taking over as the star – the one thing he had thought could never happen in his career. But had he been wrong? Could the same thing happen with a television show after all? Might he get a slot on camera if Mel or Sue ever got sick or took a holiday? Every day Dermot dreamed about this kind of break. He even practised a few scenes in the privacy of his bedroom at home, just as he had done as a boy back in Colchester. But in reality he knew this was a break too far. He was trapped in the Catch 22 situation of wannabe presenters. He could only go on camera if he was a well-known name. But he could only become a well-known name by going on camera. He was in his mid-twenties and thriving in front of his lunchtime audiences. But sometimes real success seemed as far away as ever.

The good news was that Dermot was at least in the right

place, and that he was surrounded by many of the right people. *Light Lunch* producer Jamie Glazebrook was one of Dermot's earliest supporters, one of the first to tip him for the top, saying he had a feeling right from the start that Dermot deserved a bigger audience. Dermot meanwhile said 'He's the nicest boss I've had' about the man who is now famous for Channel 4's *The IT Crowd*.

On a wider level, Dermot knew he had been right to move on from the rarefied world of documentary making in Hammersmith to the mainstream world of daytime television on the South Bank. *Light Lunch* itself may have gone off the boil fast and may not be well remembered today. But at the time it was at the vanguard of a real sea-change in British television. Today, critics say the whole of the 1990s was pretty much a golden age for live television. Johnny Vaughan and Denise Van Outen on *The Big Breakfast*, Chris Evans on *TFI Friday* – shows like *So Graham Norton* and *The 11 O'Clock Show*, which launched the careers of Sacha Baron Cohen, Ricky Gervais and Mackenzie Crook. Then there was a new army of talent including the likes of Jamie Theakston, Ant and Dec, Cat Deeley and Zoe Ball (who like Dermot had gone from a runner to a researcher on her way to the screen).

All these shows and presenters were developing in a hot-house atmosphere where everyone knew everyone else and nobody was afraid to gamble. Television historians say the industry was on a roll with all the old certainties about who should go on screen and when being torn up and re-written for the new age. The late 1990s were the most exciting of times and the television rollercoaster was starting to hit a whole series of new heights. Could Dermot get on board for the ride of his life?

THE WARM-UP MAN

In many ways, Dermot knew he was ideally placed for to make the leap. Gregor Cameron, one of the brains behind *The Big Breakfast* back in 1992, sums up what broadcasters wanted back then. When he looks back to the way his show worked he inadvertently ended up giving a perfect description of the attitude, and background, of one Dermot O'Leary. 'Live TV begins and ends with the talent, and that generation of presenters were all people who had done their homework with the TV on. That generation was the first one that had grown up with TV in such a way that they were able to break the rules. It was something that was imbued in them that previous generations didn't have. The presenters and the producers all knew that people were savvy to the underlying nuts and bolts of television. So the programmes showed you the cameramen and the lights. We all just pulled the walls down and made the shows a bit of a sitcom.'

Dermot certainly wanted a starring role in one of them.

He was fizzing with enthusiasm about Channel 4. He had found out just how insidious the television world is and how quickly it gets under your skin. 'Being in a television studio is like a drug, you are always left craving for more,' is how one insider puts it. Dermot's experience proved the point. Five years before, as a first-year media studies student, he would have given anything to be on the inside as a researcher and a warm-up man. Now these roles were no longer enough. He wanted to perform when the cameras were rolling, not just while the angles were being set up.

Now he wanted to be the host that the celebrity guests actually spoke to, not just the person who booked their appearances and arranged their taxis home.

But how could he get onto the next rung of the career ladder?

His time on *Light Lunch* seemed to pass in the blink of an eye. Like every other freelancer in television Dermot was soon looking for another contract. But this time he was setting his sights high. He decided not to go for another relatively easy-to-find job as a researcher or even as a warm-up man on another show. It was time to make the leap in front of the cameras. He knew it might take some doing – and he might be unemployed for a while as he waited for the right opportunity. But fortunately he was sharing a flat in south-east London with his big sister (and her two cats, Nelson and Edgar). This flat would be the springboard for his career. And the clock was ticking. This would be a very good time to get the job of his dreams!

In late 1997 Dermot recorded his first proper show reel, a television 'calling card' that he could send out to producers so they could see him at work. Filming this made him realise that he definitely was cut out for television. He really was. 'The first moment the camera light went on I knew this was what I wanted to do,' he says of those early sessions in front of a camera. It was a moment of total self-realisation and absolute clarity. The clean-living Irishman had found his drug of choice. The young boy who had been taken to see Terry Wogan all those years ago had never given up on his dreams. He still wanted to be in front of the cameras himself. So he set about making it happen.

After his clip reel had been polished up he sent it out to as many producers and production companies as possible. He read every advert in *Broadcast* magazine and he put the word out with everyone he had ever met in the industry that he was up for a new challenge. He rang up agents, agencies, broadcasters and producers. But for every step forward he seemed to have to take several steps back. If he had thought that becoming a runner or a researcher was tough then this was torture.

In the months ahead he did screen test after screen test and turned up for audition after audition. But the call-backs never came. And after a while the doubts started to seep in.

Dermot remembers that his first few screen tests were a mixed bag – at best. Often he looked around the studio, past the cameras to the (often non-existent) crew the way his heroes like Jonathan Ross and Chris Evans always did. But was this too mannered, too forced? Should he buckle down and keep his eyes on the camera lens? Should he make love to the camera or treat it all like a giant joke? A show reel gave him the chance to try all different approaches and decide which looked the best. But in the late 1990s he went through agonies of indecision when it came to including, or editing out, each individual clip. Would he ever get it right?

Two men would change everything. First was producer Phil Parsons; second was the former CBBC and *Live and Kicking* presenter Andi Peters.

Dermot sent his show reel to Phil back in 1998 and for once it was noticed. (Television insiders say most unsolicited show reels aren't even watched, let alone acted upon. That is especially true if, like Dermot, you don't have a high-powered agent pushing your case to potential employers.) Phil's interest was a turning point. He called Dermot up and asked him in to work on a couple of pilot shows that the producers were hoping to sell to mainstream broadcasters.

Sounds good? It wasn't necessarily so. Pilots can be a soul-destroying business. You want to do your very best and put everything you have into the show. But after a few failures you wonder if anyone will ever see your work or if it is ever really worth doing. Dermot didn't quite get this cynical in the late 1990s. He liked making new contacts on the shows and he knew he still had a huge amount to learn. But he did start to feel desperate. So near, but so far. Those were the five words that haunted him in 1998 and beyond, as so many doors around him stood ajar, but stubbornly refused to open wide enough to let him through.

Of course he wasn't alone. Dozens, hundreds in fact, of others were buzzing around the outskirts of the industry all convinced that they had that elusive 'X factor'.

One of the contacts he did meet as he did the rounds of auditions and pilot shows was fellow wannabe Melanie Sykes, whose career was just about to hit the heights. The pair both worked with Phil on a youth show that never quite made it. And just before they were told that no one was taking up the option to turn it into a series Dermot got some good news. He won a few freelance shifts on the BBC's kids show *Fully Booked*. The Sunday morning programme was on a real roll when Dermot signed up. Its high profile proved the point that kids TV, far from being a backwater, was the hottest place to be. 'These were boom times for children's television and a huge amount of talent was being nurtured there,' says presenter Andrew Miller, who made his name on the Channel 4 programme *Boon!* 'When that generation of presenters was growing up all you could aspire to was being a *Blue Peter* presenter and working within the very strict format of that show. By end of the 1990s the amount of children's programming had soared and the programmes were pushing the boundaries and making a lot of people in the industry pay attention.'

So *Fully Booked* was a perfect place for Dermot. And his first major commission for the show could hardly have been more exciting. 'Dermot, you're going to Los Angeles. And pack a bag now because you're leaving tomorrow.'

For an Irish boy from Essex this trip was an incredible experience. It was the first time he had been out to the west coast of America and the first time he had ever been put in an all-expenses-paid hotel room. It felt like the big time from the moment he checked in at Heathrow – not least because the ticket had been booked so recently that it was hideously expensive. Most people would have had a pang of doubt at this point. They'd have looked at the figure on the ticket and wonder if they were really worth that much money. They'd worry about letting everyone down if they weren't. The pressure, already sky high, would have become stratospheric!

Amazingly, the expensive plane ticket was only the beginning. Even being in a ritzy LA hotel was just the sideshow. The job Dermot had to do out there was terrifyingly high profile – he had been lined up to interview Gary Oldman, Heather Graham, and Matt LeBlanc from *Friends*. These were among the biggest names in show business back then. Speaking to them was a huge responsibility. The fact that *Fully*

Booked had won the interviews was a huge achievement. But what if Dermot blew it all by freezing up, messing up or otherwise screwing up? He is the first to admit it was a baptism of fire and that he spent his first day in LA 'sweating and worrying' in his hotel room while he waited to be told exactly when and where the interviews would take place. If he was nervous, then he certainly survived.

He met his crew and headed to another hotel where the interview guests were on a media tour speaking to presenters and crews from around the world. Dermot and his team sat and waited for their turn. When it came he reckons he did a great job. And interestingly enough he believes he learned one other valuable lesson, one that would stand him in good stead in the years ahead when he met and interviewed many other stars on his other shows, which was that it isn't necessary to be terrified of meeting the stars themselves. 'It's the entourage with the stars that's more intimidating,' he said afterwards. 'The celebrities themselves are either quite nice or quite boring. Gary Oldman was one of the nicest people I've ever interviewed so that was a great way to start out.' He remembers he also thought Matt LeBlanc was so laid back he could have become a good mate, while Heather Graham was, well, just the sexiest woman he had ever seen.

So could anyone on Dermot's 747 have been feeling any better as he flew back to London, mission accomplished in LA? He certainly didn't need to be at 35,000 feet to be on a high. Sure, the *Fully Booked* job had only been a small freelance gig. But he was convinced it could be the first of many. And being in the jet set wasn't a bad feeling either. He headed back to his sister's flat convinced that the phone was about to start ringing off the hook.

Unfortunately, it didn't.

His celebrity interviews went air on *Fully Booked* and seemed just as good as any others on the show. But still the employment drought went on – and that can trigger a whole host of insecurities. A rookie presenter would be forgiven for worrying. Had the producers been lying when they said I did OK? Had they really thought I had made a connection with the guests? Was I really their first choice for that interview or did I only get it because everyone else in the world was busy? Everyone in the TV business knows that what producers tell the talent to their faces can be very different from what they say in the privacy of the production offices or the editing suites.

Everyone desperate to be on television must worry sometimes. Every hopeful presenter must wonder if they were the reason for the stubborn refusal of their phone to ring. Am I too tall or too short? Am I too young or too old? Have I got the right look for today or am I already out of date?

Questions, questions – and there are precious few comforting answers. Many hopefuls in the media have phases when they become more rather than less nervous as time goes by. Instead of gaining confidence with each new job they seem to be losing it. In such a tense, precarious world it's all the more heart-wrenching to realise that when Dermot got his next big break he very nearly blew it.

CHAPTER 5

MEETING MARGHERITA

'**H**ello, I'm Dermot.'

'Hi there, I'm Margherita.'

Neither of the two nervous hopeful presenters knew that a great new television double act was about to be born. And neither did any of the production staff around them.

The scene was a small, independently run film studio where yet another pilot programme was being put together. It was a place where Dermot's insecurities would be on full display and where Margherita Taylor nearly despaired of her surprisingly tense new co-star. The happy-go-lucky creature we all know today certainly wasn't in evidence back then. 'The pilot was for a sports show called *No Balls Allowed* and it felt like a really long day because it really wasn't working between us,' Margherita remembers.

'Dermot is a perfectionist so we kept having to do things over and over again.' But this desire to get things right wasn't the thing that worried Margherita most about the handsome Irishman at her side. What bothered her more was what he did when things went wrong. 'When he couldn't remember a line he'd hit his head really hard with a shoe. I didn't know him at that point and so it scared me.' It got the wind up most of the other people in the studio as well. Obviously Dermot was either just very nervous or a very big joker. But hitting yourself on the head with a shoe? Isn't that all just a little bit too extreme?

Dermot himself smiles ruefully when he thinks back to that tense all-day shoot. He admits that he wasn't just nervous of the job in hand he was intimidated by his beautiful young co-star. At that point, Margherita had been a regular face on shows like on *Videotec* and had hosted several shows on Capital Radio. She wasn't just a wannabe. She was on her way, a star-in-the-making. 'I didn't feel star struck when I met Margherita but there was a certain pressure, especially when you're trying to get a job,' he admits.

And the shoe incident?

'My Achilles hell has always been learning lines so it was essentially a day of self-flagellation. I went away thinking: a) I haven't got the job and b) I'm never going to work again because this girl who is already on the inside thinks I'm a lunatic.'

He was right on the last point. 'I certainly didn't think we would ever see each other again,' Margherita laughs.

But see each other they did. *No Balls Allowed* got a green light. It was the first of Dermot's many pilot shows to get a production deal. The money was lousy – the show's entire budget was less than the catering bill on a typical prime-time BBC drama. But in some ways that worked to everyone's advantage. 'The lack of money meant we really had to rough it and that certainly brought Dermot and I closer together,' says Margherita. It also helped create the on-screen chemistry that would get the pair noticed. 'We would meet up night after night, just panicking. It was mutual fear that brought us together,' says Dermot with a big smile.

Mutual fear or not, the end result was good. *No Balls Allowed* didn't exactly trouble the judges at Bafta time that year. Nor, to be fair, did it have many viewers rushing to set the video recorders on at home. But for Dermot and Margherita it was still the perfect place to be. It was both a testing ground and a springboard. They took full advantage.

'The beauty was that it was a new show that allowed us to make mistakes, and it just got better,' he said. He loved the production meetings, even the post mortems after bad shows. He was keen to write as much of his own scripts as possible – and the producers were keen to let him if this saved money on other writers and allowed them to use their micro-budget in other areas. Dermot found that all his years at the coal-face of TV, as a runner, researcher and warm-up man, stood him in good stead. The skills he had learned in those low-rent jobs meant he had an instinctive feel for what the producers – and the audience – wanted to see.

More exciting still was the fact that he found he could deliver on these instincts. Yes, he often talked too fast – he still does, he knows it. Yes, he could sometimes drive people nuts by forgetting or ignoring his script and going off on a brief tangent – he still does that as well. But no one could deny that this stocky, short-haired young man had some sort of spark. The cameras loved him. So was he finally on his way? This was when Andi Peters came in.

Andi Peters had a tough job to do. Channel 4 wanted to go for the youth market in a big new way. They had picked him to get them results – and fast. Andi was the man who had become a kids' TV star at the Beeb. He had found a happy home in the 'broom cupboard' of early morning TV. But he had tired of being on screen, convinced that real creativity – and better money – could be made off camera as an executive. Now he had made that move and was a production company boss building a reputation as an unlikely visionary – and a very tough taskmaster.

The one bit of good news about Andi's new job was that Channel 4 had some great new shows to broadcast in its prime Saturday and Sunday slots. It was importing some cool new series from America to run alongside teen soap opera *Hollyoaks* and the best of British. What the broadcaster wanted was a solid structure to hang all these shows around. And it wanted a whole new identity for the weekend slots.

Andi's idea was that Channel 4 would morph into *T4* to achieve his bosses' goals. The 'T' was nominally a short-hand for teenage. But Andi and his team were always looking a little beyond that demographic. They wanted to bring in everyone from 16-year-old school kids through students to twentysomething young professionals. If a few older viewers got the bug too, then all the better. But what kind of presenter would appeal to such a diverse crowd? Andi's vision for *T4* was presenter-led from the start. He knew he needed the right faces to bring the brand alive. He never expected them to be easy to find.

The concept launched with Essex-boy and *The Bigger Breakfast* graduate Ben Shephard in the hot seat doing the 'morning after the night before' job. He was on screen from mid-morning till mid-afternoon, introducing the likes of *Hollyoaks*, *Dawson's Creek* and *Planet Pop*. He did the live links and the unscripted interviews with the latest pop stars, soap stars and a fair few desperate wannabes. And if Ben hadn't taken a two-week holiday then that's how the *T4* story might have ended. But he did take that break. And Andi chose two young pretenders to fill in for him. They were Dermot and Margherita, living proof that you don't necessarily need tens of millions of people watching your shows to reach the top: you just need one very important person to watch it and see your potential.

Andi was convinced that Dermot and Margherita had the right chemistry for *T4*. He had seen them on *No Balls Allowed* and felt they deserved better material. So he got them back together, gave them their two-week slot and watched the screens light up.

'You were just great. Thank you so much.' When Ben came back from his holiday Dermot and Margherita were let go. But when Ben then decided to move on in 2000 they got an immediate call-back. Andi says he never had any doubts that they should be the show's new joint hosts. Nor did he doubt that when they got back on screen they would start to make *T4* their own. Fans described the pair as a sort of 'human Sellotape' that helped bind the whole mass of programmes and strands together and made it work. And while Dermot is more than a year older than Ben he somehow manages to seem younger on screen. And younger – and cooler – was what the producers really wanted. So Dermot could hardly have been a better replacement.

Audiences loved the show's new look and feel. And they adored Dermot.

'Dermot had this easy, seemingly effortless ability to be on the side of the viewer. He really was the best mate all the blokes watching wanted to have. And he was the guy the girls wanted to be with. It was the prefect combination. He didn't threaten anyone. And what was most interesting of all was that even he didn't realise how good he was at all of it. He didn't realise that he was a natural. He didn't know that he was cool,' says long-term fan Andy Newing. This effortless charm, and subtle edge, helped Dermot turn Channel 4's weekend line-up into the hip, elder brother to the likes of *Live and Kicking* and *SM:tv*. In the process, he helped create a whole new vibe for a whole new set of viewers. It was television for the slackers, for the duvet generation whose tastes and demands were a lot sharper than they might appear.

Students in particular seemed to love the show. The original idea for *T4* might have been to target those in their mid-teens. But it was soon all but a set text at most universities – and while he didn't know it at the time, one student in particular was watching when Dermot first took to the air. Her name was Dee Koppang – and when they finally started dating many years later he says it was 'a bit of a mind melt' to think that they had connected so much sooner than he had ever thought.

Dee's fellow students must surely find it equally wonderful to think that she has ended up on the arm of the man they all laughed alongside and even lusted after all those years ago. At the time very few girls anywhere would have thought Dee or anyone else might end up with Dermot – because everyone assumed he was happily dating Margherita.

The on-screen chemistry that Andi had spotted was getting stronger with every passing weekend. The old breakfast television station TV-am had famously said it wanted its presenters to have 'the F-factor'. Whether this stood for 'fanciability' (as TV-am claimed) or something a little more basic, it was clear that on Channel 4 Dermot and Margherita had it by the bucket load. The crew were all well aware that both presenters were single. So was there really love in the air?

'By the time we did *T4* we both knew each other inside and out,' says Margherita, who maintains they were only ever just good friends. And for their first six months on the show she reckons they were too focused on the programme to consider anything else. 'We both really wanted *T4* to work. We were both really passionate about what we did so we would put in the extra hours, make sure we knew the script backwards and work on making it funnier and more creative all the time. The banter was the way we were in real life and we then became these two exaggerated characters on screen. Dermot would muck things up and I'd tell him off and everyone seemed to like it.'

Dermot in particular certainly liked her attitude. He loved it when she checked whether he had learned his lines – just like his mum had always checked whether he had done his homework back in Essex. He reckoned there was a real school ma'am, Mary Poppins side to her character – a matriarchal edge that kept him happily on his toes.

'There's no sexual tension. We have a very natural friendship. I look at her and think she looks fabulous, but I never once think I'll ask her out. It would be like sleeping with your sister. She's actually like my sister, my girlfriend and my mother all rolled into one,' he said when he was asked about the 'are they or aren't they' relationship rumours.

The critics soon fell in love with it all as well. 'Dermot and Margherita have joined seamlessly to become the one personality that nurses the hangover, eases the comedown, soothes the headache. They're fresh so you don't have to be,' wrote journalist Paul Flynn in one of the first reviews of *T4* and one of the first reviews Dermot had ever had.

He certainly agreed that he and Margherita made a winning team – the Ant and Dec of Channel 4 and the Phil and Fern of their generation. They both felt that they brought different, but equally important gifts to the partnership. 'She's my safety net. When we go out live, we back each other up. She'll always pick up where I leave off. I act like a football manager to her, and her to me. We're always giving each other little hugs. We bring out the best in each other. She's taught me a lot about professionalism and I hope I've taught her to enjoy it a bit more,' was how he put it.

'We relate to our audience because if we weren't on the show we're the kind of people who would be watching. We're mates who have a laugh with each other presenting to groups of mates who want a laugh themselves. That's why it works.'

Margherita couldn't have agreed more. 'When you're live in front of a couple of million people you need to make sure the person next to you is going to cover your back if you get it wrong. Dermot knows how I'm going to finish a sentence, and how I'm going to start it. I trust him 100 per cent.'

The trust was essential because in the early days of *T4* the pair had some ground-breaking work to do. Taking phone calls and streaming texts from viewers is commonplace now. But it wasn't when Dermot and Margherita kicked it off on *T4* – and realised just how few of the comments they would receive were suitable for broadcast. Trying to edit out the swear words as they came in became second nature. Knowing how to stay on the right side of the line between entertainingly offensive and downright slanderous was just as important.

For Dermot this was part and parcel of the real joy of *T4*: the fact that it was broadcast live. That was what he had wanted to do ever since he had seen Terry Wogan in the flesh some two decades earlier. It was what he had loved about his few BBC Essex radio shows. It was what gave him a rush when he had stood in front of three hundred people at a *Light Lunch* warm-up. Live television is a high-wire act, presenting without a safety net. Not everyone can cope with the challenge. Not everyone can make it look easy. But Dermot could and did. Until he started at *T4* he hadn't known just how much of a buzz the job would provide. He hadn't known how much he would hunger for it all week. From Sunday night to Saturday morning he would find his mind full of ideas and jokes and concepts for the show.

Unfortunately he also found his mind full of worries and all his old insecurities. Live television certainly isn't as easy as it all might look. Dermot's hero, Jonathan Ross, admitted that he felt physically sick before early editions of *The Last*

Resort. And Dermot would go through similar panics as his star began to rise. He didn't just dream about Sunday's *T4* every Saturday night, for example – he had nightmares about it. 'I dream of imaginary guests that I don't know will be on and I wake up sweating and run across the bedroom to check the script to calm myself down,' he said. He would have terrors about drying up, with no questions to ask and no idea who was sitting opposite him in the studio. Filling in for two or three minutes when a link breaks down and a video feed comes in late might not sound like the most difficult thing in the world to do. But ask any television professional and they will say that time passes very slowly indeed when you know several million people are watching you sweat under the lights. 'Try it and see. Look at your watch and talk, right now, for three minutes if you think television presenters don't deserve their salaries,' says one household name news presenter whose own high wage has brought in plenty of criticism in recent years.

Dermot, who jokes that he is an Irishman who can talk for England, was always able to pull a few minutes' worth of anecdotes out of the bag when required. So as the weekends passed, so too did the stress. After six months he told pals he had never been happier. 'I feel more comfortable in the studio doing the show than I do just sitting at home,' he said. But interestingly enough he didn't always feel comfortable with the one side effect of his new role: fame.

By now Dermot was front row and central in the public eye. He was no longer just the good-looking runner or researcher who stood alongside all the other telly wannabes. He wasn't just the presenter on one-off pilot shows that immediately disappeared without trace. He was the star of a television phenomenon, in the youth market which had suddenly become the highest-profile battleground in broadcasting. He also looked fantastic – so the Channel 4 publicity staff understandably wanted to make the most of him.

In a few quiet moments some older and wiser members of the production team warned Dermot that his life was about to change dramatically as interest in him grew. He told them that the transformation had already begun. He was first aware of it when he went out with friends, family, or on a very rare date. His good looks had always turned a few heads. But this was now premier league stuff – and its effects went beyond just Dermot. 'It is all a bit weird when someone comes up to you in a restaurant and asks for your autograph but completely ignores the person you're with or is rude to them. That's hard to get used to – for me or for the person I'm with,' he said.

His next challenge as public property was to overcome his natural reserve and succumb to the hair and make-up staff and the stylists in a series of photographic studios. Channel 4 and *T4* understandably wanted plenty of images of their young host to be available to the media. And then they wanted to give the papers a lot more opportunities to use them. They wanted Dermot to climb on board the standard publicity bandwagon and give as many press interviews as his diary allowed. This was where it could all have gone horribly wrong. For Dermot didn't want to play ball. 'Maybe I'm naïve, but I don't see why my work shouldn't do the talking,' he told pals. It was millennium time and the cult of the personality – of the celebrity – was gaining ever more ground. But Dermot didn't want to be part of it. So after a huge amount of soul searching he agreed to a limited number of profiles and interviews – though he reserved the right to refuse to say a word about his past, his personal life, his family or his background.

Years later almost everyone in the television industry laughed away at the Christmas 2007 episode of *Extras* where the Ricky Gervais character tries to take on a whole new, supposedly sophisticated and intelligent, persona for a disastrous fictional interview with a broadsheet journalist. Dermot long since seems to have realised that you can't get away with putting on an act for the press like that.

Fortunately Dermot proved to be a total charmer in all the early interviews he did give. Reporter Charlotte Moore remembers interviewing him for *Marie Claire* just after he hit the screens. 'He bounded Tiggerishly around looking for somewhere comfy to chat,' she says of the meeting. 'He was friendly, flirty and cheeky,' she says. No change there then. But he was also something else: he was a lot brighter than his interrogator had expected. Later he admitted that all the fussing around for a couple of nice chairs was a classic displacement activity. A tiny part of him had hoped that if he took so long setting the scene there would be no time left for any questions at all. But as it turned out Charlotte did manage to pose most of her questions and the *Marie Claire* interview got a great showing in the magazine. And that mattered. The magazine's key readers – largely professional, 20- and 30-something women – weren't natural *T4* viewers. By charming them Dermot had won a whole new set of fans.

But even so it took nearly a whole year before he agreed to do a new series of big set-piece interviews. As each one got ticked off his list, he started to relax a little more about it all. He almost enjoyed meeting some of the reporters – sometimes he would happily stay chatting long after the allotted time for the profile had ended. But he still stuck to the lines he had drawn in the sand. He had decided that he wouldn't take the headline-grabbing route of washing any dirty linen in public – even if he had had any to wash. He wouldn't talk about sex or girlfriends, real or imaginary. He wanted to retain his dignity, and hope that people then respected his privacy. Luckily for him he was able to do all this with a smile.

All the reporters who met him in the *T4* years agreed that there was something very special about Dermot. 'He's very tactile, but not in a slimy way,' said Jo Carnegie, formerly of *Heat* magazine. 'Sure, he has that extra drive and self-confidence associated with someone famous. But if we could imagine any celebrity as "One Of Us" then it would be Dermot,' she says. Having said that, she couldn't help feeling that if Dermot really was just another one of our close pals he might talk a little more about the passions and the loves of his life. Jo remembers that she found him cagey in the extreme. 'He's a contradiction. One of the most friendly but enigmatic celebrities around,' she concluded.

Dermot himself was well aware that he was bucking the celebrity trend. And that he did need to throw the media the occasional bone to generate publicity both for himself and his shows. The reality of the modern media was not going to be lost on the man who had a degree in the subject, after all.

'Everyone deserves a private life but you get paid a disproportionate amount of money and you enjoy a certain lifestyle and with that comes an opportunity cost. And that is losing some of your privacy,' he told *Heat* magazine in May 2002. And to be fair, he reckons that at the time he couldn't have had a wild, tabloid-friendly life even he'd wanted to. He had already stopped going to Saturday afternoon Arsenal games because he couldn't trust himself not to head to the pub with his mates afterwards. And as for late, late nights? Forget it. Being on *T4* was almost as bad as being on breakfast television for the early starts. And while it began as a two-days-a-week job it did extend into three for Bank Holidays and then lasted all week in the school holidays.

Dermot said his big fear was coming over as 'Mr O'Bleary' if he ever went out for one too many the night before a show. Losing his edge by being hungover or tired would be unfair on himself, on Margherita, on the production team and on the viewers. And anyway, forget the 'oh poor me' po-faced stuff. Dermot didn't want to be hungover because he was having too much fun sober. Forget celebrity girlfriends, even. Dermot was getting quite enough out of his relationship with the cameras.

'On live television, the buck stops with you. You get sweatier palms, but it's an ego trip – you know you're in charge of the channel for half an hour or whatever it is. No point in denying it. That's a real turn on,' he declared about this new love of his life. And his clean living regime didn't mean that Dermot was a total goodie two shoes on the set. He didn't feel he needed to be. So when disaster struck he was always the first to smile and carry on. 'People don't want to see an automaton. They like it when things go wrong – I do. People want to know that presenters have a human side, they want to know that we're fallible and we can laugh at ourselves when we have to.'

The other secret to Dermot's early success was the fact that he had never forgotten the faces of the first few studio audiences he had warmed up for Mel and Sue, what now felt like a thousand lifetimes ago. He didn't forget that those same sorts of people were now watching him from home. These memories affected the way he saw himself and the job he thought he had to do. 'I'm not the star of a show. I see myself as working on behalf of the audience, to bring them closer to the real pop star or the actor or whoever. I love making a whole studio laugh. I think if I've done that then I must have made people laugh at home as well. That's what TV is all about.'

But TV was also about stars. And however much he tried to deny it, Dermot was the clear star of the *T4* show. Even the feisty, music-loving Margherita was soon edged slightly into the sidelines as Dermot's confidence, and fan base, grew. Viewers said a key fact in his slow takeover of the show was that he didn't just interview boy bands – he looked good enough to be in one (though they also pointed out that if he was in a band then he would be the moody, cooler guy at the end of the line, not the needy, desperate one singing in the middle, a comment that made Dermot laugh out loud when he heard it).

It was the same with all the comments and articles describing him as 'TV's new hunk' or 'Irish babe magnet Dermot O'Leary'. No one, it seemed, did self-deprecation quite like Dermot. 'Why am I a heart-throb? Because the kind of people watching are hungover and haven't put their contact lenses in yet,' he said with his wide, trademark smile. He also tried to push away the idea that he was getting bigger than his show. 'It's the ideas that count on a show like *T4*, not who's on screen presenting them,' he claimed. But in truth it did matter who presented them. And as usual, when he is pressed, Dermot is well aware of the work he did and of the value he gave the channel. The self-deprecation only went so far. 'Sure, it was just a links show,' he said of *T4* several years later. 'But it was of its time and it succeeded through word of mouth, which is a real achievement. Other shows have huge marketing budgets to rely upon. We succeeded solely because of the work we did on screen.'

Perhaps this latter point meant the most to him. Respect and recognition from his peers was hugely important to Dermot; it always had been. His solid, hard-working parents had always made him fear the television was a trivial, lightweight career option. He had always worried that people might think he did a frivolous job in an insubstantial industry. So while he could never pretend that a television show for hungover students was as tough as coal-mining or as important as something like medicine, he vowed that he could at least prove he did the job that he had as well, if not better, than anyone else. Ratings alone don't prove this in the entertainment industry. The real proof that you've made it comes in extended contracts and new job offers.

Dermot was about to be given both.

In the summer of 1999 he got the call to join the team on *The Bigger Breakfast*, the longer-running version of the main

The Big Breakfast show that was broadcast in school holidays, on Bank Holidays and a few other one-off occasions. The offer was a huge confidence and credibility boost for Dermot. And the show itself was the perfect fit for him. With a particularly wide audience – including the very young and, perhaps surprisingly, the very old – he could be even more relaxed and have even more fun than he did on *T4*. So if that meant dressing up in ridiculous costumes (the chicken suit was his favourite) then that was what he would do. Whatever the producers thought would work, Dermot was ready to do. And they remember that he was always there ready to pitch ideas of his own into the pot to keep the show fresh. The show was a madhouse, most days. Dermot loved being given a key to the asylum.

And there was something else. For Dermot *The Bigger Breakfast* didn't just mean a wider audience, more fun, more experience and more money – though all four were accepted with thanks. Nor did it simply mean the chance to have his name ranked alongside other *Big* and *Bigger Breakfast* hosts such as Josie D'Arby, Ben Shephard and old pal Melanie Sykes. No, the final selling point for him was that the show was filmed live. It confirmed that this was where he wanted his future to be.

Over the past few years he had often gone behind the scenes or even sat in the audience of other shows that his pals were making. When these programmes were live he had to hold himself back, he was so desperate to leap out his seat and join the fun on set. But when the shows were being broadcast he felt strangely flat. There was something about the fact that you could do re-takes, and rely on the magic of editors, that took the passion out of the performance. That wouldn't stop him doing recorded shows himself if he was asked. But it would stop him from enjoying them very much

'There's nothing about live TV that I don't like,' he says. 'I don't even care if I make a fool of myself when things go wrong.' And that was just as well. Because in those first few years an awful lot did.

CHAPTER 6

LEARNING FAST

Insiders say that up-and-coming television stars need a very thick skin to survive in this most brutal of industries. They need to cope with irrational rejections and endless auditions. They need to see people with less talent make much more money and climb the career ladder far faster than they themselves do. They need to ignore ugly words from professional critics and cat calls in the street from jealous members of the public. They need to paint on a smile and fight, even when they feel like hiding away from the world and giving up altogether.

They also need to be able to bounce back fast if things don't go well on the set.

Dermot learned this final lesson pretty early. If he'd thought he had the whole celebrity interview thing sussed after his first successful meetings with Matt LeBlanc, Heather Graham and Gary Oldman for *Fully Booked* then he was about to get a shock. He was about to meet Mick Hucknall. Things seemed to go badly from the start. But who was to blame? If he has learned one thing in his time in television, it is never to lash out at the runners or researchers for things which may not have been entirely in their control. But he feels that someone, somehow, had led Mick into believing he was to be interviewed by some beautiful *T4* babe. He thinks the pop star clammed up once he realised he was sitting next to a squat, sturdy bloke with big arms, super-short hair and stubble.

Dermot fans all say they hope that one day someone leaks the interview footage and posts it on YouTube. In the meantime, all they – and Dermot – remember are awkward silences, short answers and difficult pauses. For Dermot the experience was a useful wake-up call – a reminder that he couldn't afford to coast and expect every guest to be media-trained, media-friendly and ready to please. It made him add an extra section to his pre-interview researches – to find a few extra avenues to walk down should his guest clam up on all the most obvious approaches.

Funnily enough, Dermot would get even more food for thought a few years after this infamously bad interview. He was surfing the web at home one day when he stumbled on a website that promised to list 'The 1,000 people more irritating than Mick Hucknall'. Thinking it would be a bit of a laugh he clicked on to it. And saw his own name worryingly high up on the list. 'Talentless C4 twat' was the first comment from the person who had nominated him for the list. 'One of a list of f***-wit celebs who I'd like to beat with a spade.'

This initial comment appeared to have opened the floodgates to a whole tide of anti-Dermot abuse.

'He's a midget' said one anonymous writer. 'With a very annoying, shouty gravely voice' said another. 'His back of the throat drone is crucifying,' added someone else. 'He is a talentless gutter TV host' said another. 'Why can't he sit still for more than 30 seconds? Why is he always wriggling and jerking his head around? Is there something the matter with him?' asked another. 'Boring, boring, boring, bland, bland, bland. Couldn't Channel 4 have found someone with a pulse or a life?' asked another. And so it went on...

Sitting in front of those full screens of criticism hit Dermot hard. It was the first time he had really faced such hostility. The first time he had realised how cruel the internet could be. 'It does knock you back,' he admitted, more sensitive and less thick-skinned than he had hoped to be. 'You're on TV so you can't help but acknowledge that you are slightly driven by your ego'. His was certainly hurting as he scrolled down the comments and read the worst reviews of his life.

What he then decided to do was to ignore them – after a great run as TV's new, bright young thing he knew that some sort of backlash was inevitable. A much older colleague had told him something important way back at his old Hammersmith offices when he had been working on some of the company's documentary projects. 'When it comes to reviews you either read and believe everything or nothing,' the old-timer had said. 'If you believe in your good reviews then you won't be able to dismiss the bad. The only way to laugh off the bad ones is to treat the good ones as jokes as well.' It had been a tough and complicated lesson for Dermot to take on board back then, several years before he even made it on to the screen. But now it seemed to be just the moment to dust the words down and try and learn from them.

'Always let your work do your talking for you,' was the other big 'rule to live by' that Dermot had picked up along the way. So that got him through the mini-backlash as well. And the producers and crews he worked with did still like what he did.

They particularly appreciated how good he was at thinking on his feet when things went wrong on air. Fortunately, like many Geminis, Dermot reckons he's a good man to have around in a crisis. And he also believes he learned a lot from the Mick Hucknall debacle. He proved it one day when he was interviewing the actor Joshua Jackson. A few minutes into the live chat he realised his guest's microphone had either fallen off or wasn't working. No one could hear what the man was saying. So Dermot jumped up and sat on his guest's knee so they could both talk into his microphone instead. 'It was a crazy thing to do and you probably can't imagine Parky doing something like that. But for me, for *T4*, it worked,' he says with a trademark big smile.

One other weekend he decided to talk about his sister's cat when a video was slow to play and several empty minutes needed to be filled. Another time he stood up and danced, for no obvious reason at all, when a similar gap needed to be plugged. It was almost vaudeville in its comic effect. And it worked. These were the kinds of things that got Dermot talked about behind the scenes in the broadcasting world. They were the kinds of things that could win him a lot of new work.

One of the next people to come up with an offer was Barry Ryan, head of the independent production company Straight TV. It had won a commission to produce a new weekly magazine format show showcasing the dance, music and club scene on Ibiza. The show needed to be ice cool. It had a very tongue-in-cheek provisional title: *The Dog's Balearics*. What it needed was a credible, personable, flexible host. Barry says that from the very start there was only one name in the frame. It was Dermot – and Barry had some very interesting reasons for making that choice.

'Why Dermot? I wanted someone with their own unique take on what's going on. Dermot's expertise and skill is that he isn't actually a presenter at all. He's a human being. He's perfect for *The Dog's Balearics* because he isn't an anorak and he isn't part of any tribe.' In essence this was the same reason that had got Dermot his role on *T4* – if he hadn't been presenting the show, he was exactly the kind of person who might be watching it. And as with *T4* Dermot would be twinned with an equally cool female co-host, this time former model Jayne Middlemiss. 'Dermot gels perfectly with Jayne. They are television gold-dust, like Richard Burton and Elizabeth Taylor' said Barry, with his tongue firmly in his cheek, yet again.

But exaggeration or not, Barry knew what he was talking about. He knew his audience – and the universe of potential presenters – inside and out. He knew what worked and why. Here's what he thought: 'There have been so many presenters that I have worked with and you walk down the street with them and people shout: "Ugh! Wanker!" When we started the show I walked through the streets of Manchester with Dermot and everyone was going: "Alwright, Dermot, how's it going?" And it's not just the girls who want to be photographed with him. He gets mobbed by boys in exactly the same way as a footballer.'

Dermot was back on a roll. The regular trips out to Ibiza were a fantastic bonus. The chance to do music television cleverly extended his fan base yet again. Meeting and interviewing stars like Boy George was fantastic. And the female dancers on the beaches and in all the clubs? They were pretty good to have around as well. 'This really is the dog's balearics,' was his feeling as he got into the swing of the show. All this and a nice fee for the work. Could life get any better when you're young, free, single and on TV?

As he pondered the question, Dermot was about to get a wake-up call – a reminder that if life couldn't get much better it could certainly get worse. He, Barry, Jayne and the rest of the Straight TV crew were loving their new gig. But the critics weren't prepared to be kind. Many of the early reviews of *The Dog's Balearics* were bad – and Dermot had forgotten his recent vow never to read them. But with the negative words still buzzing around his head Dermot knew he couldn't afford to be thrown off his game. For he had an even bigger one-off gig just around the corner. It too would bring its fair share of professional and personal triumphs and disasters.

The job was his first major commentary role. He was picked to talk viewers through the vast Party in the Park in London's Hyde Park in 2000. Police figures put the crowd in the park at 100,000 while Channel 4 was aiming to get at least three million watching across the country. It was Dermot's biggest stage to date – and his longest on-air job. In total, he had to be ready to talk for up to 12 hours when all the pre- and post-show segments were added up. And few of them passed easily. The show was bedevilled with a seemingly endless series of technical problems and glitches. There were non-functioning mikes, non-available video links – and then there was the problem with Elton John's piano.

Dermot himself never really knew what the issue was. He just knew that Elton wasn't on stage when expected. And that no one knew when he might arrive. Dermot had only a few lines of introduction jotted down on his pad for Elton's arrival. They only took a matter of seconds to say. Then the ad-libbing had to begin. And it had to go on and on. Dermot's Irish gift of the gab was put to its sternest test yet. And to this day he visibly cringes at the thought of some of the things he may have said. After the show he was given a set of tapes so that he could see the whole concert from the viewers' point of view. He has watched a lot of it. But he has never found the strength to listen to the run up to Elton's set.

Still, who cares about a bit of aimless on-air rambling when you're surrounded by beautiful women, right?

Dermot is surely too much of a gentleman to say or even think it – but in Hyde Park he had plenty of stunning Irish girls to focus on. He and fellow commentator Ben Shephard had spent much of the previous day at rehearsals play fighting over who might get to interview Andrea Corr and, as an afterthought, the rest of The Corrs. Ben won. 'I ended up interviewing Chris Tarrant instead. Where's the justice in that?' Dermot jokes. But he still reckoned he had a chance with Andrea. 'I had to do a link at the end of Ben's interview with the girls and I kept thinking, "Say something really funny in front of them and Andrea will fall into your arms." In the end I came out with, "Well, thanks for having us, lads". They just looked at me blankly. In fact, Andrea didn't look at me at all.'

What's one of the big perks of being on TV? Getting paid to meet beautiful women has to be high on the list – even though in Dermot's case he sometimes made a fool of himself in their company, as he admits he did with Andrea Corr! For a sporty boy from Essex it was still a marvellous way to live. And the party wasn't over yet. As his next big gig, co-presenting *The Clothes Show Live* in Birmingham, would prove. Dermot had been picked as one of the hosts of the show alongside the far more famous – and far taller – Jamie Theakston. The pair sat in a very public commentary box to talk the crowds through the catwalk shows and speak to many of the models. They also went out into the crowds to chat to audience members and help do a bit of star-spotting.

It was great fun, not least because Dermot and Jamie were good pals from the start. 'We get on unbelievably, shockingly well. Normally it takes two weeks of so of knowing someone before you suss them out but Jamie and I got on like a house on fire from the first moment.' They had a laugh, trying to chat up some of the snootier models, but mainly they just worked hard for the audience, desperate to keep things fresh for the sixth identical catwalk show of the day. Jamie was also broadcasting his radio show from the venue and Dermot was pushed back into his old warm-up role – though it barely went much better than that first day with Mel and Sue.

'I was there to do the warm up and the announcer yelled out: "Ladies and gentlemen please welcome Dermot O'Leary" and I swear they all went: "Who?" which made the team all laugh.' But he soon got noticed. After a while he started to love it. 'Basically, I go on stage and 7,000 girls scream at me. That's not a bad feeling', he admits. Especially as he was being paid for it.

This final point is interesting. For Dermot was about to show how different he was to almost all his broadcasting peers. Forget turning up at the opening of an envelope. Dermot was becoming known as 'Dr No'. He was young, handsome and could have been the hottest property in town. He could have paid off his mortgage with a few randomly chosen jobs. But he turned down far more than he ever accepted. He might always be smiling. But he was very serious about wanting a long-term career.

So just after his *Clothes Show Live* outing he said no to a big money Beckham-style job as an underwear model. 'I just don't see myself as a sex symbol. I know how I look when I get out of bed in the morning,' he protested. Legions of female – and some male – fans tried hard to persuade him otherwise. But he had no intention of changing his mind. It was the same with the vastly lucrative corporate and awards merry-go-round. He has done a few big events over the years – notably the *Elle* Style Awards in 2005. But he has rarely felt comfortable. His view seems to be that nights out are for spending in the pub with your true mates, not for air-kissing with beautiful strangers in the ballroom of an anonymous five-star hotel. So he has done far fewer of these gigs than many of his peers. Jonathan Ross, Jimmy Carr and a small band of other big name presenters have made small fortunes on the awards circuit. Dermot has never followed in those particular footsteps.

'Can't we find Dermot a celebrity girlfriend? Can we get the paparazzi to get some shots of him outside a nightclub pretty soon? And why the hell doesn't he go to nightclubs anyway?'

In 2000 those were the kind of questions those cynics in the media might have asked as whole armies of people prepared to join the O'Leary bandwagon. A hot young TV star could make a lot of money for a lot of people. But only if he wanted to play the celebrity game. And all indications showed that Dermot did not. 'Sure, there's a little bit in all of us that wants to be famous, isn't there?' he admitted when he was quizzed about his motives for being on TV in the first place. But he wouldn't sell his soul to further his career. Within the media he was already becoming known for his refusal to go on the record with any details about his private life. Even a group of trainee reporters for *The National Student Magazine* noticed how keen he was to do anything other than discuss his life away from the cameras.

The students had been asked to sit in on a publicity photo shoot for Channel 4 and had been promised a no-holds-barred chat afterwards. They didn't really get it. 'He's totally charming but he is permanently off getting the stylist a drink, introducing himself to the assembled crew or talking football to the photographer's assistant. Actually getting him to sit down and do a proper interview is virtually impossible,' remembers one of them, correctly diagnosing it as the displacement activity that has always worked so well for Dermot when he wants to shy away from tough questions.

It was pretty much the same with the minders and the publicity staff at Channel 4 itself. He remembers that they were constantly trying to have him 'media trained' before his promotional interviews. But Dermot was convinced that 'media trained' was actually code for 'transformed into a media tart'. Charming as ever, he always turned them down.

Interestingly enough, Dermot didn't just want to keep a low profile because he wanted to protect his family and friends from the media spotlight. Nor was it because he quite frankly thought his life was too dull to really interest people. Another key reason was his appreciation of the way the celebrity world worked. He had a theory that as a man he could play the long game in his career. This was what his old hero Terry Wogan had done. It was what his new hero Jonathan Ross appeared to be doing. It was what Dermot himself wanted to try.

'The shelf life for a male presenter is longer than for a female presenter so you don't need to worry about making as much money as you can as quickly as you can. Because you can stay working for longer, you can let your work do your talking. You don't have to milk every opportunity while you are hot because, as a woman, the media doesn't seem to like you staying hot for very long,' he says. He adds that he totally understands why so many of his female colleagues do play the fame game so voraciously. He doesn't criticise them for taking on as many product endorsements or other deals while they are on offer. Nor does he condemn them for giving the media open access to every aspect of their lives in return for a healthy, if short-term, income stream from magazine and newspaper interviews. 'I've never wanted that kind of publicity, or that kind of publicist. It's just not in my nature to be a socialite and do all the things like celebrity openings and first nights. I'd rather be down the pub with my mates.'

And in the longer term Dermot would rather be working. That way, when people stopped him in the street they could talk about something specific like his latest show. That he could cope with. What he struggled to deal with was people stopping him and then just clamming up like the star-struck teenager he had once been himself. That was how so many people acted around his high-profile female co-presenters. He didn't want the contagion to spread to him.

But like it or not, he was about to find out that he had risen further through the celebrity ranks than he had thought. The wake-up moment came when he was asked to present an award at the National TV Awards in 2000. 'The whole thing really freaked me out. Davina McCall was on first, then it was George Best and then me. I just thought, "No one is going to know who I am." But when I went on stage the reception blew me away. I was just like – wow!' he said afterwards.

And it wasn't just the fans and fellow famous names in the studio audience who were telling Dermot he had arrived. His mum Maria says people had started to come up to her in the street in Colchester to say they had seen him on some show or other – and that he had been fantastic. Dermot liked to joke that his dad was also getting a new lease of life out of his son's fame. 'It's hilarious because apart from documentaries and natural history he has never really been into telly. Then suddenly, now that I'm on TV, he's watching all these hip, popular culture programmes and getting a whole load of new interests.'

Having remained so close to his family Dermot always knew they would offer him a refuge – and a useful dose of reality – if the pressures of being a star ever got too much. And in 2000 a few extra factors meant that those pressures were building up with astonishing speed. According to the typical script of the local boy made good and catapulted to the top of the media tree this was where it would all start to go wrong.

CHAPTER 7
MOVING ON

Bad behaviour was all the rage when Dermot became a star. Cash, cocaine and constant exposure were a toxic new combination in the media world. Scandal stalked several of his key contemporaries – Richard Bacon had made a swift exit from *Blue Peter* after a cocaine allegation, Johnny Vaughan was revealed to have had a less than perfect past, John Leslie was on the verge of even worse allegations, and Dermot's old pal Jamie Theakston had an unlikely brush with infamy when the Sunday papers reported his visits to ageing prostitutes – the list of shame went on.

And if the 'lad culture' being celebrated by the likes of *FHM*, *Maxim*, *Loaded*, *Nuts* and *Zoo* magazines wasn't bad enough, the 'ladette culture' was introducing new ways for women to live large and hope that tomorrow looked after itself. It seemed as if too many high profile women, from ex-*EastEnders* star Daniella Westbrook to Gail Porter, Zoe Ball and Davina McCall, were all being threatened by this dangerous new zeitgeist. Even the formerly squeaky clean ex-*Blue Peter* presenter Anthea Turner shocked her fans by embarking on a high-profile affair with an old pal of her husband Peter Powell.

It was as if the old rules of good behaviour no longer applied. And the pressure to ride this new wave of infamy was intense. Far from ending a career, a drugs allegation or two could take it up to a new level. A sex scandal could produce a six-figure sum from a tabloid newspaper interview. An addiction could become a best-selling book. Bad news was good news for almost everyone concerned.

To his enormous credit, Dermot was one of the very few young, credible voices to speak out against the trends. He hated the examples his male colleagues were setting for their fans. And he particularly despised the subtle misogyny of the ladette culture. His parents had brought him up to treat women well. He couldn't bear it when so few of his contemporaries did the same – or that the women concerned didn't seem to care. 'Getting in touch with your primitive side is getting in touch with your inner arsehole,' he said when the lads culture seemed to be at its peak. 'If we want to go a bit retro and get in touch with our past then we should tap into the Cary Grant mentality. There's nothing wrong with that time when men treated women with the respect that they deserved.'

For some time Dermot's words seemed to fall on deaf ears. There were too many men behaving badly for his clean-up crusade to work. But at least he had tried. In his own heart he was glad he had spoken out. And he vowed to carry on leading by example. He swore that the name Dermot O'Leary would never be in the papers over some drugs shame or a sleazy affair.

What is interesting is that Dermot could think and say all this and still remain cool. He didn't turn into some po-faced, moralising goody two-shoes. And he achieved that by keeping things light. He might not have liked the lads' culture. But he was still happy to play the jack-the-lad card when required.

'Have you ever fancied a guest?' he was asked in one of his rare promotional interviews for the latest series of *T4*.

'Have I ever not fancied a guest?' he replied, without missing a beat.

'What's the weirdest thing you've ever been sent by a fan?'

'A pair of knickers.'

'Yuk.'

'And they were unwashed.'

'Disgusting.'

'And I'm wearing them now!'

These kinds of comments kept Dermot in the public eye as latest *T4* publicity bandwagon began to roll. By 2001 he had held together more than 1,000 hours of live television, faced down all manner of production hiccups and headaches. He felt he had travelled a long way from on-screen rookie. But as the *T4* roadshow got ready for its latest launch, only Dermot knew was that this was the last time it would move with him on board. He had done a whole lot of thinking earlier that year. He was feeling more focused, ambitious and confident than ever before. He knew that *T4* had taught and given him a huge amount. But now he had big new plans. After nearly three years winning the war for weekend viewers (while simultaneously working on plenty of other shows) Dermot wanted new challenges. He wanted to test himself in tougher waters and play on an even bigger stage elsewhere.

To the producer's dismay he asked for a top-secret meeting. Everyone sat down, one team member got ready to take notes and then Dermot said it. 'Guys, I'm sorry but I think it's time I moved on.'

Dermot didn't resign from the *T4* in a huff, nor did he flounce out in a diva-like fit. He certainly didn't let anyone down or try to cut short his contract. But when his commitment to the show came up for renewal at the end of that summer he made it clear that he was saying goodbye for good. He felt it was time 'I've learned as much as I can from *T4* and I think I've taken the show as far as I can,' he said.

Interestingly enough Dermot wasn't walking into entirely uncharted territory here. Many years earlier his old mentor, Terry Wogan, had unwittingly shown him the way. 'He did *Wogan* three times a week for seven years and then he bowed out of the show of his own accord and on his own terms. That's class,' said Dermot as he prepared to do the same thing, albeit on a far less high-profile scale, in 2001. When he dropped his bombshell, the *T4* producers realised there was no point in arguing. In private they agreed that they had hung on to their star for as long as they could reasonably have hoped. They knew he was doing the right thing.

For his part, Dermot did have a few wobbles as he filmed his last series of *T4*. Life as a freelance television presenter doesn't hold many guarantees. If you work, you can earn great money. But if the phone stops ringing, that cash might have to last a little longer than you had originally planned.

This realisation pretty much explains Dermot's rare slight misjudgement of that year: the M&M's advert where he pretended to interview a set of round, over-sized sweets lined up on a *T4*-style sofa. He had been speaking into thin air and the giant M&M's were added later in the editing suite. It was high-tech stuff back then. It wasn't exactly *Star Wars* quality, but at least Dermot could relax afterwards, safe in the knowledge that the advert wouldn't be around forever.

How wrong he was.

The wonder of YouTube has given this low point in his career a new lease of life. His most woeful of performances can be seen on demand. To date, more than 7,000 people have watched it on the site. Very few of the comments make pleasant reading – some of the early ones making the point that the plastic sweets are more animated than their host.

A shame-faced Dermot has since admitted that he couldn't even blame too many other people for the humiliation of the advert – not least because he co-wrote most of the silly script himself. 'Look, a boy's got to eat,' he joked when his pals took the mickey out of him. And that boy also had a new set of big bills to pay. He had finally moved out of his sister's flat and bought his own house in Queens Park, north London – a traditional Irish stronghold where he had a local that served a perfect pint of Guinness less than 600 metres from his new front door.

The M&M's job had given him the money for the deposit on that house. But it hadn't stretched much further. At 28 years old Dermot knew he was gambling big time. And as a lifelong worrier he didn't sleep that easily when he thought about it. 'I'm paranoid that I won't be working in six months and won't be able to afford my mortgage,' he told *GQ*'s Niki Browes, who met up with him just after he had handed in his notice at *T4*. She remembers that Dermot was also worried about the future on a more personal level. Each series of *T4* had been made by pretty much the same crew each and every week – a relative rarity in the high-turnover world of TV. Dermot would miss all his old colleagues – and he kept nagging at them to make sure he would still be able to join in their occasional football games in Regent's Park. As a joke, they all said he couldn't. Though when he called their bluff and turned up one evening he was of course welcomed with open arms.

The crew also had a couple of surprises for his very last show on the programme. Spice Girls mania might have been on the wane, but Dermot, like very many other 20-something men, still reckoned he was in love with Baby Spice, Emma Bunton. Getting her as his final guest was his first leaving present. Having her turn the tables and interview him rather than the other way around was his second big surprise. In truth, she didn't exactly have any killer questions to ask. And Dermot wasn't so off balance that he revealed any juicy new facts about his life. But everyone had a laugh and the show ended on a high.

But what would happen next? Had Dermot made a huge mistake by willingly jumping from one of the hottest shows on TV? Some commentators rushed to say that he had. Their theory was that Dermot was simply a big fish in the small pond of youth programming. They predicted that he would flounder and die in the cruel seas of mainstream, prime-time television.

But for a while at least, it certainly seemed as if Channel 4 still wanted to keep him – while ITV and the BBC were both very keen to woo him. This was 2001, the age of the multi-million golden handcuffs deal that was increasingly on offer to the best presenters as well as the highest-profile soap names. Big money was being put on the table for Dermot. Long-term contracts were being drawn up. But Dermot was about to surprise everyone – especially those who simply saw him as a genial jack-the-lad who lacked the killer career touch.

'Thanks. But no thanks.' That was pretty much what he told the paymasters at all three of our biggest television stations. Dermot was thrilled to be in such high demand. He was dazzled by the amount of cash the programmers were willing to pay for him. But he didn't feel old enough to be tied down. He didn't want to be forced to do programmes he didn't like, just to fulfil a contractual obligation he should never had signed in the first place. And in the years ahead he would thank his lucky stars for sticking to his guns. Like others, he watched with interest as the likes of Julian Clary and even Graham Norton appeared to be shoe-horned into certain shows simply to appease the people who had tied them into their exclusive contracts. Dermot had never wanted to short-change himself, or his viewers, by doing shows he didn't believe in, heart and soul.

So, free from *T4*, he wanted to play the field. For a brief moment there was a chance that he could replace Johnny Vaughan in *The Big Breakfast* hot seat – a great job for Dermot, who had enjoyed his time on *The Bigger Breakfast* earlier in his career. 'He can't match Johnny Vaughan's stream of consciousness chat, but his career is on a similar trajectory,' said *Guardian* online reporter Akin Ojumu, who was one of the few to meet him as he weighed up all his new career options that summer. He believed that Dermot could take his pick of any plumb job that year. But he emphasised how important it would be to choose well. Dermot couldn't have put it better himself.

'I don't want my star to burn out too quickly,' he said. 'The most important thing is doing the right shows at the right time. Not jumping ahead of yourself. You don't want to be on everything, all the time, or people lose respect for you.' But there was one final point Dermot had left unsaid: that you do want to be on some shows, at least some of the time, or people forget all about you.

But at least he had a game plan, back in the summer of 2001. He wasn't quite as vulnerable as he was letting on. Dermot never was. For the past few months he had been having some informal chats with a team of independent producers about a television show that had been the shock hit of the previous summer. It was the show that would carry on making headlines for the foreseeable future. It was, of course, *Big Brother*.

On 14 July 2000, more than three million viewers had watched the likes of Anna Nolan, Sadia Walkington, Mel Hill, 'nasty' Nick Bateman, and eventual winner Craig Phillips walk into a specially constructed house in east London. When that first show went on air no one knew for certain if the British public would get it. No one knew if anyone would watch, which was, of course, part of the show's initial charm. But watch we did. Talk we did. Obsess we did.

That being the case, by 2001 there was never any doubt that a second series of *Big Brother* would hit the screens. And with new television channels being launched all the time, there was advertising revenue aplenty and demand for ever-more *Big Brother* programmes so that the brand could be extended far and wide. The crucial thing was to ensure that everyone connected to the show shared those cool, young, edgy brand values. Main host Davina McCall certainly did. And the executives at *Big Brother* producer Endemol reckoned Dermot did as well. So as the next set of as yet unknown housemates got ready to enter a new house that second summer, Dermot got ready to help us get to know them. *Big Brother* was already a television phenomenon. We were about to meet its Little Brother.

CHAPTER 8

HELLO BIG BROTHER

'**W**otcha, do we have the best job in the world or what?' Dermot didn't even try to hide his excitement as the first episode of *Big Brother's Little Brother* hit the screens in May 2001. Those were his first words to camera as the initial, typically manic, show got underway. From then on nothing seemed to stand still for a moment. Dermot fired off an endless set of his now trademark head jerks and salutes to the cameras. He made near constant references to the crew who were shadowing his every move. He darted inside and outside the set. And he never stopped moving or smiling. He and co-host Natalie Casey were like happy little kids let loose in the celebrity sweetshop.

'A lot of people would pay a lot of cold hard cash to be here,' Dermot said as he sat on the soon-to-be-famous *BBLB* sofa, in front of the bank of 49 television monitors showing more than 30 live feeds from inside the house. It would turn out to be one of the hottest sofas of the summer. 'We give you the stories as they break and let you air your own grievances,' he said. But there was much more to *BBLB* than that. What worked most was the way Dermot and Natalie opened a window into the previously unseen *Big Brother* world. They readily had the cameras turned around to show the producers, the secret rooms and the innermost nuts and bolts of the programme.

The premise was the logical conclusion of all the in-joke TV that had begun with Jonathan Ross and Chris Evans and pulsed through all of *T4* – the turning of the tables that allowed the viewer to see how a show was made. Dermot was clearly the best guide around.

And from the start he certainly looked better than almost any other man on television. His face was fresh and alive. His body got noticed. The material of his shirts always seemed to be stretched by what were soon dubbed 'the beefiest arms on television'. And he always seemed to be dancing right up to the edge of the line of public decency. Somehow he knew just how far he could go when discussing – or insulting – the housemates and his guests. He said what most of his viewers were thinking. But because he was always smiling and playing up for the cameras he got away with it. How can you be offended when the man doing the talking looks so mischievous and innocent? The whole gig was a rollercoaster ride of fun. And Dermot was never lost for words.

Every night he rifled through that day's papers for *Big Brother* stories. He had all the internet pages to talk about, all the texts and emails and phone messages to build into his material. He also had some choice housemates to talk about. It was the year that we got to know Bubble, Josh, Narinder, Helen and the ultimate winner Brian Dowling.

And the media obsession was intense. Newspapers had specialist '*Big Brother* correspondents'; each tried to win the mantle of 'official *Big Brother* paper'; and the new set of celebrity magazines all rushed to bring out commentary columns on the show – often producing a lifeline of extra revenue for former stars whose 15 minutes of fame had long since expired.

But for all the fun and frivolity, *Big Brother* was a multi-million pound generating television industry. For Dermot and co., watching it would be serious stuff. And in that second year it would prove harder than the first. 'This year they are far more media savvy, they're far more aware of what they're doing most of the time,' he said in week one of that series. 'But when you are being watched for twenty-four hours a day seven days a week you're going to let your guard down.' Dermot's new job was to be there and report on it when they did.

What also gave *BBLB* its edge was its inspired choice of great guests. Everyone on the production team thought laterally every day. Who might have a new angle or edge on the latest events? Who would have something new to say? Who would make us all laugh? Friends and family of the housemates were only the start. Anyone connected to them could also get an invite and end up sitting alongside Dermot and Natalie. They also called in the psychologists and psychiatrists, the body language experts, the lip readers, the soothsayers – you name it, Dermot wanted it. And if it all got a little over the top then Dermot never shied away from saying so. His arch glances to the cameras and ad lib comments when he thought someone was talking nonsense were hilarious to watch. They always made one key fact clear: Dermot's on the side of the audience. If you think something's gone too far then so will he.

What he also grew to love were the hecklers in the audience, all the people who spiced things up by shouting out if they thought he was being unfair to their favourite housemates (or, sometimes, if they thought he wasn't being unfair enough). Jamie Nairn, then a media studies student, who was on the show in 2001 to support Penny Ellis, says Dermot himself was clearly the hub of the action. 'If he was reading a script at all it certainly wasn't just one that someone else had written for him and put on his autocue. He was permanently writing things down as the show got ready to air and he was always making notes in the commercial breaks as well. He did take time to welcome everyone on the show before we went live and he seemed to be as nice as you would have imagined. But when the show actually began he seemed to really come alive. He was flying. You could kind of tell that the people behind the scenes were a bit nervous about where he might go or what he might say. But that tension was probably what made the show so watchable. It felt like seat-of-the-pants stuff. Dermot's skill was to hold it all together.'

When asked, Dermot totally agreed that he wasn't some passive script-reading telly clone. 'I'm doing my own thing. I'm not in any way a television presenter in the traditional sense,' he said. But he wouldn't sell himself short either. 'You can teach any idiot – well, most people – how to do pre-recorded television,' he said. 'But live TV needs a certain smartness.' Dermot is quietly proud to possess this vital smartness. In spades. He reckons he has long since worked out what makes a good presenter. And he knew he could deliver that as well. 'It's about being yourself. It's a cliché but it's like hosting a party and there are two million people in your house and you make sure they've all got a drink and you must be not intellectual but intelligent. You've got to be funny, without being a comedian.'

The professionals agreed that Dermot got it all pitch perfect.

'He's cute, but he's not just an auto-cutie,' was how one *BBLB* staffer put it. So the whole experience it was perfect for him. Madcap, seemingly unplanned, constantly off-message. And broadcast live, ultimately six times a week, and normally with Dermot dashing around the studio fired up by adrenaline and barely drawing breath. Most of the time he clutched the clipboard he called 'my comfort blanket', and he never sat still for as much as an instant. He was always physical, always animated, his face going from grin to grimace, from smile to frown in a heartbeat 'I love it and I get paid well for it. Can life get much better?' he asked his mates.

And when the first few reviews of the programme started to filter through Dermot realised that this time life could get a little better. The critics loved him. He was soon dubbed 'top boy, in the cool school of television presenters'. He might one day call *BBLB* 'a backstreet little squirt of a show', but it could certainly punch well above its weight. And then one day something else happened that made Dermot realise he really was on the edge of the big time. It was mid-afternoon when his mobile rang. A number he didn't recognise was flashing up on the screen so he answered warily – and found himself talking to Jonathan Ross.

Does life get much better than this? Dermot was asking himself yet again as he spoke to his professional role model and one of his all-time television heroes. And once again Dermot found out that life could get better. Jonathan invited him round for dinner.

'He has the biggest house in the world,' Dermot told his mates after the big night. He had bangers and mash, onions, gravy and baked beans, all served up by Jonathan's wife Jane. And all night the talk had been about Dermot's favourite subject – television. Jonathan is famously knowledgeable about television trivia. Years earlier he had been one of the first people in his leafy north-London street to install a huge satellite dish so he could watch – and learn from – television programmes around the world. Just like Dermot, Jonathan is a big fan of the long-standing American chat-show hosts and entertainers. He was constantly analysing what makes one show work and another one fail. He also knows everyone who is anyone in the television industry. Dermot left the dinner feeling he had been breathing truly rarefied air. He also felt invigorated to know that he wasn't quite alone in being so fascinated by popular TV.

The only cloud on the horizon was the fact that the *BBLB* gig was by definition a short-term arrangement. When Brian Dowling emerged as the second *Big Brother* winner it was time to pull the curtain down on the show. Everyone expected there to be a third series the following year. But would the show's 'little brother' be around to snap at its heels again? And what would Dermot do in the meantime?

The phone didn't ring at Dermot's home. Nor did it ring that often at his agents' offices. But the man himself wasn't particularly bothered. He had a sleep debt to pay off. And he was very relaxed about the future.

The big benefit of high level television work is that you can earn enough on one show to see you through most of a year. If you keep your expenses down – which the debt-fearing Dermot always did – then you really don't need to worry about money for a very long time. The trick, say the insiders, is to ensure you have always got a signed contract for a new show in the bag when each old show ends. It doesn't matter if the new one won't start for many months. As long as you know it's set in stone then you – and your bank manager – can relax.

So Dermot did manage to relax. He worked out at his suburban, north-west London gym, he re-joined a group of his mates on a five-a-side football team in Regent's Park, and he watched hour after hour of tapes of his favourite UK and US shows to try and pin down what it was that the presenters did to hold everyone's attention so well. One of his colleagues explains: 'Dermot has a surprisingly broad knowledge of other shows overseas as well as in the UK. He watched David Letterman, Jay Leno, Geraldo, Ricki Lake. We're guessing he also practiced some of their mannerisms in the privacy of his own home to see if they might work for him. He's not someone who's too arrogant to think you can't learn from others. He doesn't copy them. But he doesn't rule out learning from them. His view is simple: There's absolutely nothing wrong with wanting to be the best at your job. And there's nothing wrong with learning from the masters.'

By the early summer of 2002 he had learned a lot of these important lessons. And it paid off – big time. For that year he wasn't just back on screen in *BBLB*. He was back as the show's sole host. Presenting alongside Natalie Casey had been a blast the previous year. Dermot always thrived with feisty women at his side. But what a compliment to be told he had the presence to carry the whole show on his own.

'Dermot hit the ground running in 2002 and pretty much from the first show it was as if the whole production had always been his baby,' says critic Tom Kilbourne. 'Today very few people remember that he ever had a co-presenter at all. It is the mark of a good performer if he stamps his identity so forcefully upon a show that his name is synonymous with it. That was absolutely the case with Dermot O'Leary and *Big Brother's Little Brother*. He did more than just cope on his own – he thrived.'

Tom's fellow critic Cameron Borland, reviewing *BBLB* for the influential 'Off the telly' website, clearly agreed. He argued that *BBLB* was 'easily the most user-friendly of all the *Big Brother* shows', and that this was largely due to the skills of the 'increasingly impressive' Dermot O'Leary. Here's a slice of Cameron's full review of that year.

'Forget the heavily pregnant McCall on a Friday and the nightly updates on Channel 4, just tune into Dermot and you'll receive the finished article – gaudily raucous, eminently watchable, charmingly self-deprecating and a show that positively basks in the glow of self-indulgent navel gazing. Hosted with increasing confidence and pleasurable panache, O'Leary has grown into his role with accomplished ease. The jettisoning of Natalie Casey seems to have freed the manic, agitated O'Leary from the co-host constraints he had been shackled under, and unleashed a (short-arsed) hyperactive one-man hurricane that transformed the show from a bit of a curate's egg into the raw, unfinished article that now works so well.'

In an ideal world the surprisingly sensitive Dermot could have lived without the description 'short-arsed'. But other than that he had to agree it was a critique to die for.

And in his more reflective moments Dermot felt he deserved every single positive word. That old steel was back in his voice as he showed just how much tougher he had become since taking over the reins on *BBLB*. For perhaps the first time, he was happy to say why he thought he had his new role – and why some of his so-called rivals would never manage to steal it from him. 'I enjoy what I do and I know I'm good at it,' he says. 'Of course I've been lucky. But success is about three things: luck, talent and hard work. You can be as lucky as you like but if you haven't got the talent and you're not willing to work hard then you won't succeed. There is so much bad television out there and so many bad presenters. It's hard to find good presenters for the simple reason that most people are presenters because they want to be famous and the rest are presenters because they can't do anything else.'

They were tough words from Dermot, and a rare public criticism of his peers. But Dermot did have something to get off his chest, now he was finally a blue chip success. It was a nagging desire to speak out against all the doubters he had faced off as a runner, researcher and general TV dogsbody. 'The nicest thing about climbing the ladder is that you almost want to flip the bird to all the people who didn't support you when you started out,' was how he put it in 2001.

'Flip the bird? So would you actually do that?' he was asked. 'Of course I wouldn't,' he replied, his nice guy Dr Jekyll now back in front of his rarely seen Mr Hyde. 'But it's nice to know you can if you want to.'

Insults aside, Dermot was well aware that he had managed to find his industry's holy grail – the ability to mix the enthusiasm of a fan with the slickness of a television professional. And he could do it six nights a week, three months a year. No wonder his confidence levels finally caught up with his ability.

Of course in 2002 Dermot and the whole *BBLB* crew did have some help as they set out to become must-see TV. This was *Big Brother 3* – the wildest, most popular year yet with a seemingly endless amount of madness to dissect every night. It was the year that Kate Lawler won the show, but when Jade Goody became its biggest star of all. It was the year that 'East Angular', 'minging' and 'kebab bellies' became catch phrases; when 'will they/won't they' questions about sex in the house became 'did they/didn't they'; and when every few hours seemed to bring yet another brilliant new drama. *Big Brother* has rarely been better, say its keenest fans. And alongside it all, talking it all through, every step of the way, was Dermot.

'You want me to wear what? This has to be a joke. Oh, please

no.' Over the years 'dressing up Dermot' became a huge part
of the fun for *BBLB*'s surprisingly stable production team.
The costume, props, hair and make-up staff says life behind
the scenes was never dull – because life in front of the
cameras was always wild.

Dermot's crazy costumes were a huge part of the show's
fun. 'You check your pride in at the door. I'll do and I'll wear
whatever anyone wants,' he said as each series got underway.
Then, and in the years ahead, favourite outfits among his
fans include the George Galloway leotard, the Kylie outfit,
the kangaroo suit, the return of the chicken costumes – the
list can go on and on. Few of these outfits were dignified,
fewer still were flattering and quite a number were a little
more revealing than Dermot had thought. 'Dermot, I can see
things,' Davina once said pointedly when he interviewed her
in one show wearing a white jump suit that was a little too
tight in a few crucial places.

'I'm sick of you dressing me up to look like a total idiot,'
Dermot shouted out behind the scenes at the start of most
shows – the words would become a trademark and in early
2008 he would say them for the final time when he
ultimately left the series. But of course he loved playing the
fool. The more ridiculous the clothes, the better, he said. And
if he could dance away while dressed up as anything from a
cheerleader to a space man then so much the better.

The crew also had a ball doing plenty of 'green screen' work
where Dermot's mouth and words were spliced on to the
housemates' faces to give a very different take on what was
going on in the house. Throw in the time-travel machines and
all the other gimmicks and it's easy to see why some of the

BBLB staff said they were so happy they would almost work there for free. Well, almost.

Ultimately, *BBLB* would prove that Dermot was embarrassment proof. Which was just as well – because at one point after his second series he did make a rare gaffe. He was with one of his co-workers having a nose around the empty house the day after Kate had been unveiled as the winner. Dermot and his pal had been talking about the kind of girls they fancied, and Dermot had carried on the conversation from what he thought had been the privacy of the housemates' loo. Of all people Dermot should have know that the words 'housemates' and 'privacy' don't ever go in the same sentence. And he got a sharp reminder when a young, panic-stricken runner dashed into the house to tell his boss that the 24-hour internet feeds were still turned on and that Dermot's thoughts – and the soundtrack to his pee – were about to enter internet folklore. Fortunately for Dermot, that is one clip that has yet to appear on YouTube. Though he knows it's probably just a matter of time.

In future years he could have been excused this kind of mistake because he was so tired all the time. There was a period when the last of his hour-long shows didn't go on air until 11.30pm. However brief everyone tried to keep the daily post-mortem on the show, it was always approaching 2am before Dermot got to leave the Elstree Studios and head back to north London.

Years ago he had happily sacrificed his Saturday afternoon Arsenal games and the Friday and Saturday nights at the pub in order to ensure that the *T4* shows went well. Now he was running out of things to give up. And he struggled to live a normal life. For a long time, when he felt as if he was working seven days a week, he says his recently-bought home resembled a monastery. 'It's got nothing in it because I don't have time to buy anything. It's a real bachelor pad, but that's not out of choice,' he said. For the first six months he didn't even have a fridge – but when he was unable to keep milk long enough to make himself a cup of coffee in the morning he realised he had to get his act together and at least attempt to buy a few basics.

Since then he has grown surprisingly keen on modern furniture. His home is something of a design shrine, though he steers well clear of anything that even vaguely resembles a 'diary room chair'. Billie Piper famously said she asked the BBC production team if she could have a Dalek to put in her hall when she left *Doctor Who*. Dermot pointedly didn't want any links to his studios in his north London house – not least because when he was there in those early *BBLB* years he couldn't switch off from the show as it was. He made notes about it at his kitchen table, and dreamed about it in bed. And he had plenty of classified material to dream about. He loved the fact that as an insider he could see and hear all the naughty bits that can't be broadcast – from the showers scenes to the libellous comments that can't go in any transcript. He says that the people – and there have always been a lot of them – who criticise the show tend to fall into two camps. Either they haven't really watched the programme, or they are in denial about the kind of country we all live in. 'Come on, the British love sitting on their arses and doing nothing. We're such a domestic nation and our curtains are always twitching. That's why *Big Brother* works,' he said. And that was why he was riding the wave of public fascination. That was why he was suddenly such hot broadcasting property.

By the time he had made *BBLB* his own he was earning great money doing the job he had always dreamed of. He was getting to meet fascinating people on a near daily basis. He had the approval and support of the vast majority of his professional peers. On almost any level Dermot O'Leary had it all. Didn't he?

CHAPTER 9

IN THE MOOD FOR LOVE?

He was young, handsome, rich, successful and a big star on TV. So why the heck was Dermot so cagey about his love life? Why was he almost always on his own?

The girls from *Heat*, *Marie Claire*, *Closer* and all of the tabloids had tried to get the answers to these kinds of questions from him ever since he had hit the screens on *T4* and *The Dog's Balaerics* years earlier. None of them had managed to get anywhere. Several had seen their own extracurricular advances politely rebuffed. Colleagues on his shows also agreed that in romantic terms he was easily the darkest horse in the stable. So what was going on? Was this charming Irishman some kind of monk?

In a way he was – as Dermot was the first to admit.

'What word describes you better than any other?' he was asked, time and time again in the early years of his fame. That is the standard question that pops up in so many of the 'personality questionnaires' that celebrities fill out for their publicists. Most people use the question as a chance to show off. 'Brave', 'Relaxed' or 'Passionate' are all common replies. Dermot was different. 'Celibate,' he said, with barely a hit of a smile. And it wasn't a one-off, throwaway remark.

'Can you describe yourself in four words,' he was then asked as part of a different interview questionnaire with one of the Sunday magazines. 'Sad, sad, sad – and celibate' he said. For a 29-year-old lad-about-town it was the strangest of responses.

Stranger still was the fact that it was true.

For a while, as he tried to get his career off the ground, Dermot could just about rationalise things and say he didn't have enough time for a steady girlfriend. But he remained single for large swathes of his twenties for other reasons.

The times he had been rejected by Colchester's finest as a teenager still bothered him. He took years to shake off a sneaking suspicion that he really was the nerdy, introverted kid that the girls seemed to assume. The other lads on his football, rugby and running teams managed to trade on their sports skills. But the trick didn't seem to work for Dermot. So for too many years he was worried that there might be something else, other than just bad timing, which was holding him back. By the time he graduated from university and began work he had started to put other hurdles in his way. Everything about his solid, Irish family background told him that he too should settle down with the right girl – and stick with her for life. So he was never going to have too many one-night stands.

And as his career developed he worried even more about the motives of those around him. 'When I was a teenager I never really had girlfriends. But when I first appeared on telly suddenly the girls were all interested in me. I know I'm not the smartest guy in the world but even I could see what was going on there,' he says with a wry smile. The more he thought about this state of affairs the more worried he was about taking advantage of it. Three things bothered him. First was simple distaste. He didn't like the idea of being with a girl who was with him only because of the job he did. The second reason was practical: he didn't feel he had the energy to deal with a girl who was really just tapping him for contacts so she too could get a job in front of the cameras. The final reason was sensible. He feared being the subject of a newspaper kiss-and-tell. Too many of his peers in the youth television market had been hugely embarrassed by 'five times a night' type stories – however flattering they may have been to their egos. Dermot wanted to steer clear. So most nights he went home alone.

When he did meet women he fancied, Dermot admits that he always found it difficult – impossible even – to play it cool. He had played a long game to get his career on track. He couldn't seem to do the same with his personal life. So he would rush in, like a ridiculous puppy, he says. He would try to set up too many dates too quickly and end up scaring girls away. In his most reflective moments he wonders if back then he wasn't a little too obviously needy, too desperate to be liked. And, making it all so much worse, the kind of women he approached were the last type to respond to this 'need to be nurtured' style. He likes strong, independent and confident women. Despite his traditional Irish/Essex upbringing he had no issues with career women – it would never have occurred to him to think he had to earn more than or be more successful than his partner.

So where the hell was she?

'I've had my moments, of course I have. But they've been carefully selected moments. I wouldn't want words like "grossly unprofessional" thrown at me because I had been doing something I shouldn't have,' is all he will say now about those early years on *T4* and *BBLB*. *Sun* reporter Emma Jones remembers talking to him about the irony that he got paid to talk to some of the most beautiful women in the world – but that he couldn't seem to make the leap from interviewer to intimacy. He saw the point straight away. 'When I see presenters who end up going out with famous people I think: How did that happen?' she remembers him telling her. 'I'm really a lot more shy than I thought.'

Relationship experts say this kind of thing can create a vicious circle whereby you become so afraid of dating that you only ever ask those you are pretty certain will always turn you down. Then you can blame them, not yourself, for your single status. Dermot wasn't quite in that position. But for a while he certainly did struggle. The one girl who did say 'yes' to his request for a date was former S Club 7 singer Rachel Stevens. Dermot was beside himself with excitement – and as Rachel was off filming when he asked her he was more than happy to wait for her return before they fixed a time and place. Unfortunately, when that moment came Dermot's diary was suddenly full for a couple of weeks. It meant that the O'Leary/Stevens love match – that would have made newspaper and magazine editors jump for joy – kept being postponed. And during those unavoidable delays something happened. Rachel met the actor Jeremy Edwards, another of Dermot's close pals. Jeremy's diary wasn't so busy.

So they got together, leaving Dermot firmly on the shelf. 'I was gutted,' he said with a smile. 'It's a good job television is my real love.'

For their part, the tabloid editors seemed to have decided not to wait for Dermot to find the time for true love. They would find it for him. And if they couldn't they would simply make it up.

Over the next few years he was variously linked with everyone from Martine McCutcheon to Janet Jackson. And a cottage industry sprang up devoted to his quest for a wife. A range of: 'Born to be Mrs O'Leary' mugs and T-shirts were big sellers on eBay – they were seen as a follow-up to the 'Marry Me, Bill' T-shirts that Microsoft employees had once worn to try and catch the eye of their billionaire founder. Dermot clearly didn't have Bill Gates' fortune. But he seemed to share his appeal.

So what exactly was Dermot looking for? What kind of woman would end up on his arm – and maybe claim the ultimate 'Born to be Mrs O'Leary mug'? As he is someone who has tried so hard never to discuss his personal life in public, clues are thin on the ground. But keen Dermot-watchers picked up a few of them. 'I think confidence and independence are the most attractive qualities in anyone,' he said. He reckoned that the sexiest part of a woman's body is her stomach and once told pals his ideal woman was Sophia Loren. The pals say that if Dermot had to give a matchmaker some key words to help find his ideal woman they would be: 'fiery, passionate, sensual and independent'. He would also have ticked the boxes for 'petite girls with Mediterranean looks'. And, then, in his own words, came his final key request. 'I like a sense of humour. A girl who can laugh with me, not at me. Surely that's not too much to ask for?'

Ever the gentleman, Dermot has always kept details of his first serious girlfriend under wraps – indeed he has done the same with all the girls he has dated. In his rare interviews he won't even name the girl he began dating in 2000 – and at the time he certainly didn't want to thrust her into the limelight by taking her to a film première or having her face the paparazzi at some other red carpet event. Instead this early relationship was conducted largely in local, neighbourhood pubs and restaurants in north-west London. It developed at dinner parties and other low key events with mutual friends.

But could the relationship stay in the shadows forever? Deep down both of them probably knew that their cover would one day get blown. It was an age when photographers and journalists were desperate to break deeply personal stories. It was a time when fans demanded to know every last detail of their heroes and heroines. For whatever reason Dermot's relationship ended before these details hit the public domain. And what did he do? He bought a car!

It was a 1968 VW Karmann Ghia 1500 Coupe. 'I bought it as a spectacular piece of retail therapy after my then girlfriend dumped me. I thought fine, I'll buy a car,' he told *Daily Telegraph* motoring writer Richard Simpson for an article in 2004. The car may well have helped take Dermot's mind off women for some time. Having bought and paid for it on a whim he then threw himself into its refurbishment. He wanted the old white paintwork made black and wanted all the interiors to be restored before he took delivery. 'I'd got over the girl by the time I actually drove it,' he told Richard.

Being so focused on the new set of wheels did wonders for Dermot's 'bloke's bloke' credentials. He got a real *Top Gear* style boost when he talked about the motor – even if the experts were lining up to laugh at it.

'It's an old Beetle in drag, really. It's barely half as fast as it looks,' the Telegraph's Richard Simpson had said. Dermot was right back with a joking retort. 'So what if it a four hour journey ends up taking five hours. What's the problem?' he laughed. And so what if the rear-engine car was also prone to spins, had a totally unreliable heating system for winter and cost a fortune to maintain? Dermot loved that car. It was the first one he had ever owned and it had seen him through a very rare rough time. When he then bought another set of wheels – a nippy little Aprilia moped for zipping around town – his emotional recovery was complete. So was it time to dip a toe back into the dating pool?

It wasn't that much later that he met 'the one'. Her name was Deborah Koppang – Dee to all her friends. She and Dermot were working on different shows in the same production company offices. They saw each other often in the office corridors and – as clichéd as it may sound – around the coffee machines and courier desks. So how did the relationship really begin? David Beckham famously says he fell in love with Victoria when he saw her in a music video. When he met her he said she was exactly the girl he had hoped she would be. Could Dermot have fallen in love with Dee when he saw her at a courier desk? And would she be the girl he had hoped for a well? You'd probably need a psychologist to answer the questions properly. But as Dermot and Dee are still together so many years down the line you'd have to think something good had happened from the start. One of their first dates was in an Italian restaurant just north of London's Soho Square. It must have gone well. Dermot was some five years older than Dee – but we all know there's none of the arrogance of a star about him, nor any of the cynicism of the older man. Neither Dermot nor Dee seemed obsessed with fame for its own sake. Both were hard-working individuals. Both were proud of their roots – Dermot's in Ireland, Dee's in Norway.

Over the next few weeks and months Dermot and Dee grew closer. Whether it was work, friends or family they seemed to share the many of the same thoughts and values. Best of all was the fact that of all the people in their production company they seemed to be the only two who positively shunned the industry in the evenings.

All television insiders have easy access to a host of glitzy, and free, evenings out. They can attend a screening, a red carpet première or a show launch almost every night of the week. Whenever they want to they can head off and drink free champagne with famous names in bars, hotels and clubs.

Dermot and Dee barely seemed to do this at all.

In general the only out-of-office time they spent with colleagues was at dinner parties in each other's homes. And Dee soon found out that her boyfriend was a surprisingly good cook. Dermot apparently makes a mean smoked haddock chowder – and a few years later the Irish Stew he made on *The F-Word* with Gordon Ramsay beat the chef's own version in the weekly taste test.

Dermot was also proud to see Dee doing so well in her career. She was several years behind him on the career ladder, but she was building up a solid reputation on some troubled programmes, working long hours – and often being away from London for days at a time – on everything from Channel Four's ill-fated *RI:SE* and the equally controversial *Back To Reality* a few years down the line. Short absences didn't hinder the couple's slow-burn relationship. They seemed to help it dig foundations by giving both partners the space they required. 'As much as I miss her, there's something nice about having periods when you don't have to compromise,' Dermot said of their work-imposed absences. He certainly didn't want to miss out on a few impromptu meetings down the pub with his north London friends. Locals at several pubs near his home say he has always been a relatively regular sight in the bar, standing his rounds, not making any fuss and just fading into the background. He seemed as happy there when Dee was with him as when he was there with his mates. In general he seemed happy, full stop.

Back then one reporter described Dermot as 'the ultimate new man' in an article about modern living. But other people might have put it slightly differently. They might have just described Dermot as a gentleman – and one whose values are often rooted in the past.

'I enjoy playing the traditional role of a man', Dermot has said. 'I like paying for dinner and opening doors, not because it's something a man should do, but because it's the right thing to do. I think that women enjoy it too – but that doesn't mean that the women I open the door for isn't still my boss, or won't tell me what to do on television. I think it's a lazy argument when men say, "Well, if they want equality then they can bloody well get dinner then, can't they?" I'm of the first generation for whom it's perfectly natural for women to be your boss and you don't question it when a woman tells you want to do – which I suspect the generation of men before me did.'

They were strong words from the son of an Irish builder. But no one who knew Dermot was at all surprised that he had said them.

Locals at several pubs near his home say he has always been a relatively regular sight in the bar, standing his rounds, not making any fuss and just fading into the background. He seemed as happy there when Dee was with him as when he was there with his mates. In general he seemed happy, full stop.

So was his relationship with Dee plain sailing from the start? It soon became the longest relationship in his life.

Women, it seems, can sometimes be a little bit like buses. You wait ages for one to come along and then a whole load of them turn up at once. That seemed to be what was happening for the once-celibate Dermot. Possibly his new-found enthusiasm for life in general was making him more attractive. But whatever the reason, he suddenly seemed to be in more demand than ever. Available women seemed all around. Would Dermot give in to temptation, if only to make up for lost time?

He is happy to admit that he very nearly wavered. Monogamy, he says, 'wasn't natural for me'. But he knew it was essential for a proper relationship to function. So he didn't pick up any of the phone numbers he was given, nor did he answer any of the inviting smiles. You don't miss what you've never had, he decided. 'Before Dee it was more or less celibacy anyway,' he says. So he would hold on to what he had and not assume the grass would always be greener elsewhere. The other small speed bump in Dermot and Dee's road were the simple frustrations that come into any relationship. Every now and then little things drove one of them mad about the other. But at least they always made up. 'Sometimes I want to kill her, and vice versa, but that's inconsequential compared to the good times. In the good times it is the most wonderful relationship in the world,' he says.

What made the partnership so strong was their combined sense of fun – and their joint ability to laugh at each other and at everything that happened to them. Their first big holiday abroad together was a case in point. They went on a cycling trip around Djerba in Tunisia – and were soon in trouble. 'Dee wasn't wearing anything particularly provocative but it was a hot day,' Dermot told pals. 'We went through a little village and these children came out and waved at us, which we thought was quite endearing. Then they picked up some rocks and threw them at my girlfriend, screaming "Infidel!" at her.' Having spotted their mistake and covered up the pair started to laugh about the situation. And they have barely stopped laughing ever since.

But beyond the occasional holiday story that Dermot and Dee share with friends and family they have vowed to keep the rest of their personal lives private. Not only do they refuse to speak to the press about it, they go to great lengths not to mistakenly give the media more information than they need. Many will remember the fact that Jonathan Ross ended up getting burned when he first started dating then-journalist Jane Goldman. She had left some of their holiday photos in her desk drawer when she went out for lunch one day. Her reporter colleagues printed them in the paper. Dermot and Dee wouldn't risk that kind of exposure, though the pressure for stories – and pictures – was arguably more intense than it had been for Jonathan and Jane all those years ago. 'Dermot in love' was a big story for the tabloids and the celebrity magazines. Most were desperate for titbits of information about the couple, having found out early that full interviews would never be granted. Dermot laughed out loud at the idea of inviting a magazine into his 'beautiful home' or letting reporters and photographers join him and Dee on holiday. The pair also had quiet chats with their close pals. 'We genuinely don't want to be in the gossip columns,' they said. 'Please just give a "no comment" if anyone asks about us.'

When working out what kind of man Dermot is, it is also interesting to note who these old mates are. If you think they're famous names and fellow celebrities then think again.

Most of his best friends are old friends – though he happily makes a joke out of the situation. 'I'm friends with the same people as when I was 16 and I wasn't particularly selective then. So I'm lumbered with them,' he laughs. Interestingly enough, the small number of 'telly' friends he has are often those who won't necessarily be recognised when they are on the street. One of them is *Bo'Selecta!* star Leigh Francis, far better known as his key characters Avid Merrion and Keith Lemon. As those are the parts Leigh plays in almost all public appearances, they are the only ones that most people recognise. Dermot was one of the few to know, and like, Leigh – and his reasons for that are interesting. 'We get on very well because he's very alternative with a bit of mainstream and I'm very mainstream with a bit of alternative,' says Dermot, giving away a rare extra clue about his own surprisingly complex personality.

As the years passed it was getting increasingly more important to Dermot to have at least some sort of alternative edge to him.

But in some ways he was right to be concerned. Because when you are in the television industry, image matters and perception is all. One reviewer made him catch his breath in 2002 by describing him as: 'Far less than just a pretty face'. Others were equally harsh. 'When he is on *Big Brother's Little Brother* with all those tanned, straight haired, identikit women he really is the bland leading the blond,' ran the article. Another critic poked fun at Dermot's gym-trained body, called him a 'pumped up, jumped up presenter' and ranked him alongside all the other 'mockneys and phoneys' who dominate the media with their faux blokeish acts. That was particularly galling to Dermot. His whole career was based on being himself, even if it went against current trends. The one thing he felt he couldn't be accused of was being a fake.

And for him it wasn't enough just not being one of these people. He didn't want to go where he might meet any of them either – though this determination to keep things real could sometimes tie him up in knots.

The Met Bar, in the basement of the Metropolitan Hotel on

London's Park Lane, summed up everything Dermot didn't want to be part of. Since opening in 1997 it had been the place to go for everyone from Kate Moss and Robbie Williams. Soap stars, singers, actors, footballers, footballers' wives and wannabe-wives – for years everyone seemed to want to hang out there. Everyone except Dermot. He vowed never to go – he thought it would be mortifying to be listed in a gossip column as having been there – or worse still, photographed outside alongside a group of Z-listers or has-beens. But then he got in a total muddle after the Brit Awards on Park Lane when a group of pals all wanted to go somewhere for a drink afterwards. The Met Bar, just a few paces away, was the perfect place. But first of all Dermot said he couldn't go, because he couldn't break his vow. Then he thought he might look even more of a precious idiot if he turned his friends down for the sake of some show-business principal. So he agreed to go. And, just as he had expected, he hated everything about the place. And he's never been back.

CHAPTER 10

SPORTING BREAKS

'**S**ure. I'm in. What time do we kick off?'

If there's a football game going and Dermot's got enough time to spare, then he's there. He began playing alongside the *BBLB* production team in his second summer on the programme and has had kick-arounds with colleagues on most other shows ever since. The staff at several celebrity magazines were also shocked to find how readily he agreed to join their mini-leagues for the occasional match. A passion for sport – playing as well as watching – is a huge part of Dermot's life. Not for him is the fear that he might mess up his hair, get his hands dirty or even break a leg. Nor is there any worry about being part of a team rather than the star of the show. Dermot has been called the ultimate team player on the pitch. On the wing, in goal, in defence – he'll front up anywhere and give his best.

'Sport is in my blood,' is how he sees it. It was about to become central to the development of his career.

In 2002 he got the green light for two fantastic new programmes: *SAS: Are You Tough Enough?* and *Dermot's*

Sporting Buddies. The subject matter of the shows was the first reason why they seemed so fantastic to Dermot – of which much more later. But just as important was the fact that both would be shown on the BBC. For some time a nagging voice in Dermot's head had suggested he was trapped in some kind of 'yoof TV' ghetto on Channel 4. Could he cut it on another channel? he wanted to know. And while *Sporting Buddies* would only be shown on the little-watched and soon to be defunct BBC Choice it still felt like a great way to spread his career wings.

And anyway, two brand new shows about sport and fitness? For Dermot, what was not to like?

In *SAS: Are You Tough Enough?* Dermot took on a near Ross Kemp style tough-man role. Some described the programme as a game show. But in reality it was more of an old-fashioned challenge. The premise was to have some two dozen super-fit members of the public testing out at the SAS Regiment Training Camp in Scotland. Dermot told pals he absolutely thrived on the atmosphere up there. If he hadn't staked everything on a career in television he had always said he'd like to have been a boxer, a deep sea diver or something very physical. Now he added soldier to his list of dream jobs. He loved the camaraderie of the army. He loved the high expectations put upon all the competitors. And he was determined to live up to them himself.

Would they think he was just some sort of soft, southern television star? It turned out that they didn't. As with Ross Kemp, the real soldiers recognised something genuine in the man shadowing them. They liked and respected Dermot because he was clearly so right for the role.

The public got it as well. The show went out on BBC Two in the early spring of 2002 and while ratings were never going to set the industry alight they certainly didn't disappoint. Dermot was immediately asked back to film another series – and then another. He had carved out a great new niche – and made a nice little franchise out of being a real-life action man. In 2003 the second series, *SAS Jungle*, brought a host of new challenges. One year later, in 2004, Dermot hosted the third show in the series, *SAS Desert*, which took the competitors to some even tougher terrain. Among other things the contestants were kept awake for 48 hours in the blisteringly fierce heat. Dermot loved every minute of each show. He trained up beforehand – pounding the pavements in north London and working out in his local gym. And while he didn't compete alongside his guests on the show he did try out all the challenges when the cameras were being set up. Having just turned 30 it felt fantastic to be pushing his body to new limits. And it was all doing his career the power of good as well.

'Repeat commissions on a show like *SAS: Tough Enough* are a huge vote of confidence from the television establishment,' says producer Sarah McFarlane. 'Even if your ratings aren't sky high the fact that you are being asked back proves two things. First, that your instincts to do the show were right. Second, that the producer's instincts to employ you were equally sound. No host is ever bigger than their show. If you aren't up to scratch a new series will always get the green light without you – just ask Kate Thornton. If you get the re-commission every year then you're sending out a clear message that you're good.'

And by the time Dermot started on his second and third series of *SAS* he had already been given another indication of just how powerful he had become.

In Hollywood the holy grail for actors is to get their names 'above the title' in a movie's promotion. In television the challenge is to get your name in the title. From *Lily Savage's Blankety Blank* through to *Ant and Dec's Saturday Night Takeaway* the coronation is a rare professional honour. Dermot joined the select band with *Dermot's Sporting Buddies* in the autumn of 2002. He wasn't kidding himself that the breakthrough was as good as it sounded – BBC Choice, after all, was hardly prime-time ITV. But who cares? If nothing else the show was going to be a fantastic opportunity for Dermot to spend more time with his pals. Given half a chance, who would turn something like that down?

He and his crew went on the road filming eight shows with eight different celebrity guests. First up, when the show was broadcast in October, was, no prizes for guessing, Davina McCall. They went to see an Arsenal vs West Ham game at Highbury – and for Dermot it was a little like going home. Despite being an Arsenal fan since his childhood, Dermot hadn't made it to Highbury until his late teens. Before that most of his time in football stadiums had been spent flipping burgers in a fast-food outlet at the old Wembley. When he goes to see teams play at the new stadium now he fervently hopes that the hygiene standards have got a lot better since his day. Back then he says customers the staff didn't like – for the most trivial of reasons – really could be served buns that had been on the floor of the cabin, or worse. All sorts of nasty surprises lay in store for the rudest of the drunks. That's just one reason why waiters and waitresses in restaurants today say Dermot is a pleasure to have as a customer. He knows first hand what the price can be if you're not.

Back to Highbury with Davina… it was like being paid to do what you would choose to do anyway.

In subsequent shows Dermot went to the rugby at St Helens with Johnny Vegas, to The Derby with his former heartthrob Emma Bunton and to an ice hockey game in Belfast with Sean Hughes. The show, broadcast at 10.30pm on a midweek evening, hardly set the schedules alight. But once more this hardly mattered. Because as if having fun making and presenting it wasn't good enough, Dermot had set up a company to co-produce it alongside giant Chrysalis TV. He had been thinking about running his own production firm for some time. Jonathan Ross had done it with Generation X. Chris Evans had become hugely rich by getting involved behind the scenes of his shows. And Dermot liked the nitty gritty of television. He liked to keep his hand in with what went on behind the cameras. So Murfia was born – a word play on the idea of an entertainment based Irish mafia. Co-founded with two colleagues, Murfia had started small. *Sporting Buddies* was its biggest production to date. And it meant Dermot was able to laugh all the way to the bank as well as to the editing suites in west London where the programme was put together.

Sporting Buddies ran out of steam after its eighth show. But Dermot was keen to see if other similar themes might get the go ahead in the future. *Big Brother* had inadvertently revived his passion for football – one of the early series' sponsors was O2, which had plenty of big game tickets to give away to production staff. By 2003 this had encouraged Dermot to consider buying an Arsenal season ticket for the first time. But while the six or seven home games he got to see that season were pretty good, for someone with a girlfriend and a very busy diary it didn't seem quite enough to justify the expense. And couldn't Dermot get a job in the football industry instead?

He says ex-MTV presenter and former *Big Breakfast* researcher Tim Lovejoy has one of his dream jobs on Sky Sports' *Soccer AM* – doing a live, manic and studio-based show all built around that day's key fixtures. While he loved that show, Dermot had no illusions that sports reporting was an easy job. Like everyone else he had seen how much criticism fellow Irish heartthrob Craig Doyle had attracted when he had moved from travel shows to Olympic coverage that summer.

But at least Dermot reckoned he had credibility in a whole host of sports. Could one of those give him a new avenue to explore? American football has a long, though low, profile history of coverage on British TV. Dermot wondered if it might be time to spice it all up with a whole new show. If Tim wasn't going to let go of *Soccer AM* then could Dermot at least give 'American Football AM' a shot?

He had got into the sport back at school in Colchester where the town was ringed by several US air bases. Unlikely as it sounds, north Essex was a thriving centre for American football, ice hockey and even baseball. Dermot preferred the former and tried out for and joined several teams in his late teens – at one point he played for squads in both Colchester and nearby Ipswich, though he didn't exactly treat his US team-mates with the greatest of respect. He was always among the first to take the mickey out of them for all the padding and protection these giants of men wore on the field. There was no padding in rugby, Dermot could have pointed out. And he proved it – by getting into a rugby league that played on most of the same weekends and having to juggle a lot of training sessions and fixtures to keep all his team-mates happy.

Fast forward to 2004 and Dermot was spending a lot of time thinking about how he could pitch a new American football show. He had always supported both Miami Dolphins in the States and Colchester Gladiators in his home town. Was there any mileage in a programme that compared those two very different worlds? Ultimately, all his informal soundings of the industry said no. The sport was too much of a minority interest. 'If you want to get into sports television then try rugby – that's on the crest of a wave again,' he was told. But just like *Soccer AM* it seemed as if all the best jobs there were already taken. Dermot headed back to the terraces of London Irish as an ordinary spectator. Maybe this is the way I should leave it, he thought. Sport was his hobby. If it became his job it might lose some of its magic. And in the process he might lose even more of his precious privacy. Wrapped up in scarves and hats on the terraces Dermot remembered how good it felt to be truly anonymous. His complex love/hate relationship with fame was about to get even more complicated.

Whenever Dermot feels the pressure he pulls on his running

shoes and hits the streets. It is a throwback to his school days when he had always been desperate to win cross-country races as a teenager. Now, as an adult, he moved on to half-marathons and marathons. And while he never expected to win he did want to clock up some very good times.

He has become a regular at the London Marathon and the Great North Run – and while he jokes about being beaten by fellow racers dressed up as beef burgers and Cornish pasties he is actually fiercely proud of always finishing. Psychologists say running is a perfect pastime for ambitious, driven and uncompromising personalities, Dermot's fellow marathon runner Gordon Ramsay being a prime example. They say the sport ticks the right boxes because you aren't at the mercy of other team-mates or the random spin of a ball. Instead you are fighting just two key foes: the clock and your own determination – or lack of it. Dermot fought them both in each race. And he was particularly proud that he went below the four-hour mark in the London marathon in 2005.

On a happier note, Dermot says that in the big races there is more to a run than simply pushing your body to its limit. There's also the joy of anonymity. The joy of being lost in the crowds – something he feels most intensely in the London Marathon. 'You always have these amazing moments when someone yells out your name, not because you're on the telly but because they've just read it on the front of your shirt and they think you look a bit tired and need some encouragement. That makes me well up as well as pick up my pace. The crowds are unbelievable; it's the most good-natured event in London and it seems to bring out the best in everybody.'

When Dermot can't get lost in a crowd he likes to leave everyone behind altogether. And the more he is recognised in the street the more he likes to get away. On a rare spare weekend he often heads out to the riverbanks near his parents' home in north Essex for a few hours' fishing. As sports go it is hardly at the cutting edge of cool. But just like marathon running it ticks a lot of mental boxes for Dermot. It gives him the luxury of peace and space. It takes him back to his childhood – all those days spent fishing amid the lakes and rivers of County Wexford and in the gently rolling 'Constable country' of Essex and Suffolk. Most importantly, it lets Dermot fade into the riverbank. When he is fishing he's just another solitary figure in a hat and waterproofs. When he's fishing he's not a heartthrob or a 'personality'. And however much he loves being on television, he does need occasional breaks from all of that. Especially as his fan-base seems to be growing by the day.

'How do you feel about having such a large gay following?'

'I feel very worried about him. He should lose some weight and go follow someone else.' Dermot is the first to say that the old jokes are the best – which may well be why *'Allo 'Allo!* and *Dad's Army* are up there with *M.A.S.H* as his favourite television programmes. But he doesn't really joke about his big gay following. He loves it – and the feeling is mutual. 'Everyone loves Dermot,' says reporter Paul Flynn, who met the man for one of his very rare big interviews in the early days of his career. Having refused to speak to most of the celebrity and women's magazines which were constantly asking for interviews Dermot had surprised everyone by saying 'yes' to the request from Paul at gay magazine *Attitude*. And there was more. Dermot also agreed to go on the magazine's cover and do a day-long photo shoot to illustrate the pages inside. In the interview Dermot agreed to answer any questions at all. And Paul was hugely impressed by his candour. 'Speak to Dermot long enough and you realise he doesn't come off guard. Not because he's guarded. Quite the contrary, in fact. It's because he was never on it,' he said of one of his most easy-going interviewees.

What impressed Paul the most was that while Dermot was very clearly straight he had no problem playing along with all the 'Is he/isn't he gay?' rumours that had always swirled around him. Dermot fully accepted that people would talk, not least because he had been single for so long and tried to keep the names and pictures of girlfriends out of the press when he was dating. He also accepted that he made life easy for the conspiracy theorists. Early in his career, a famous set of paparazzi pictures of him bare-chested in a sunny London park with an unidentified and equally bare-chested male pal added fuel to the fire. Dermot was happy to wear shirts that revealed the macho Celtic cross tattoo on his left shoulder. And he was happy to joke about inspiring some dodgy dreams about the shamrock he said he had tattooed on his bum. 'I'm hardly the most beer-swilling "lad" you are ever likely to meet. I can be ten times camper than most of my gay friends when I want to be,' he says. Looking back, Dermot says he can't remember when he first realised that one of his closest pals was gay. But he does remember that it didn't ever make the slightest difference to their friendship. Today, he and Dee have plenty of other gay friends and find it hilarious that when they go out as a group, strangers often assume that he is dating one of the guys rather than Dee. 'I've got short hair and I work out, but I haven't got enough style to be gay,' he jokes when he tells people who's really dating who.

Fashion experts, both gay and straight, beg to differ on Dermot's final comment about his lack of style. They say Dermot's dress sense has had a profound effect on the way plenty of other men dress. And when pushed Dermot does admit that fashion is hugely important to him. He describes his look as 'at the smart end of casual' and that a large slice of his income is spent on clothes. As far back as 2000 he reckons he was spending up to £400 a month on new kit – and back then it was his own cash as he didn't get a clothing allowance for *T4* or any of his other shows. By the time he got on to *BBLB* and beyond he had discovered the great oddity of fame and fortune – that when you've got nothing you have to pay for everything and when you become rich people offer you things for free. Dermot's freebies rarely extended beyond the occasional offer of a new suit. But while he didn't wear the new clothes outside of the studios it was wonderful to know that if something caught his eye in a high-end magazine he could probably have it sent over that day.

He also admits to being seriously into shoes and drops some serious cash at Patrick Cox and Church's. But what he won't wear, either at work or out for an evening, are trainers. 'Nick Moran once said: "What are trainers except a load of synthetic crap glued together?" And he's right.' He takes a similar, no-holds barred approach to his T-shirts – though, as

FHM magazine's Dave McLaughlin remembers, that's not a word he likes to use. 'I don't wear T-shirts,' Dermot had told him, affecting sartorial outrage. 'My wardrobe is just a massive row of short-sleeved shirts – all from Nigel Hall.' But the Covent Garden-based Hall wasn't, in fact, the only designer label on Dermot's clothes. Over the years he had become a big fan of Nicole Farhi, Paul Smith, Gieves & Hawkes, Ozwald Boateng and a fair few other big names. For many years his fans would also be surprised to know how much he likes formal clothes. When he was on youth television and wore a 'uniform' of jeans and T-shirts (sorry, Nigel Hall short-sleeved shirts) he would often come home from work and change into his one black Jigsaw suit for the rest of the night.

Mix this self-deprecating, slightly offbeat charm with Dermot's obvious good looks and you've got the reason why his fan base was growing so fast and why he made the top tens, and often the top fives, in most of the 'sexiest Brit' charts. The editors of magazines like *Heat* found that he had the Princess Diana or the Posh and Becks effect – his face on the cover (or a teasing reference to shirtless photographs or holiday snaps) would sell magazines. Billie Piper famously said she could swim in his deep Irish eyes (he said that at 19, she was too young for him – though when she met and married the 35-year-old Chris Evans she pretty much proved he could have been in with a chance). The Wedding Channel (in a strangely unromantic survey) found that Dermot beat Brad Pitt, Prince William and David Beckham in a poll of men that women would consider cheating with. Claire Thrift of The Wedding Channel explained it perfectly. 'Brad and Becks may have the chiselled looks women love but Dermot is a real cheeky chappie who is not afraid to show his more sensitive side.'

He proved this particular point by admitting that he cries all the time – normally at films and tough television dramas, but sometimes also at anything from commercials to cartoons. And he is happy to admit to any number of foibles and insecurities. In his early days as a public figure he made one strange claim to a journalist: that he kissed the window every night before he goes to bed. 'I don't know why I've just always done it. Even when I'm drunk I don't forget,' he had said.

Today he admits that this was something of an exaggeration (and the fact that the quote was so widely printed in other profiles about him taught him to be far more careful in future interviews). But while kissing window panes wasn't a nightly ritual, he does volunteer that he often stands and looks at the sky for a few quiet moments late at night to centre himself, reflect on his position in the world and prepare himself for sleep.

Dermot also scored by avoiding the self-indulgent 'oh poor me' school of celebrity. He wouldn't act all precious and tortured and say how difficult it was being rich, famous and at the top of his chosen profession. Instead, he simply did what came naturally to him. He carried on smiling. Friends and close colleagues say that if, on any given day, you ask Dermot what he is laughing at, then nine times out of ten the reply would be: 'Myself'.

He always has a sense that his life is all a little bit crazy – that a boy from Essex shouldn't really be in his exalted company or doing so many wonderful things. And because he often feels a fool he has no problem playing the fool. He thinks it hilarious that Davina seems to tower over him in almost every joint publicity photograph they do for *Big Brother*. He never needs to be asked twice if the photographers want him to camp it up with silly faces and embarrassing poses.

Fans love it – not least because by refusing to take things too seriously he always seems to remain on our side. 'I'm not a celebrity, I'm a fan,' is how he puts it. And he admits that when he meets famous name stars he acts just the way many of us would do – like star-struck idiots. He jokes of the night he met Kylie Minogue in a restaurant – and says he couldn't breathe, let alone speak. And this was an improvement on the time he first met his original idol, Terry Wogan. That day he says he was convinced that all his blood had sunk into his legs and that he was on the point of some mortifying faint. Once more, he says he ended the meeting without having strung more than a couple of words together. Though in some ways he admits that this could have been a blessing in disguise. For reasons known only to the deepest recesses of Dermot's mind the actor Damian Lewis always brings out the foolish fan in him. And where Lewis is concerned he talks. 'Every awards show I go to I end up walking up to him and saying, "I loved you in *Band of Brothers*." And every time he looks at me as if he hasn't got a clue who I am. He's very polite, though.'

If Kylie, Terry and Damian are Dermot's show-business heroes then who are his all-time heroes? The answers help build up an even clearer picture of Dermot's true personality. They prove, yet again, that he should never be dismissed as a mere television lightweight.

The explorer Ernest Shackleton is a man who has always fascinated Dermot, though he certainly doesn't overdo the reverence. Yes, he has devoured plenty of books devoted to Shackleton's life and adventures. Yes, he loved the recent television series following in his footsteps. Yes, he thinks the man was an inspiration. But he certainly can't ignore the man's flaws. 'He was probably the world's worst explorer,' Dermot jokes, describing the infamous nearly two year-long journey across Antarctica that went from triumph to disaster and back on a near daily basis. But for all his jokes, when Dermot was asked to help launch the Antarctica exhibition at the National Maritime Museum in Greenwich in 2001 he jumped at the chance. Key attraction for Dermot wasn't just the chance to see the exhibits early and speak to their curators. What thrilled him the most was the chance to meet one of Shackleton's great grandsons.

The pair helped pull one of the explorer's boats into the museum to publicise the show and emphasise how strong the man must have been. Afterwards Dermot spent as long as he could talking to all the members of Shackleton's family who were at the event. One of them was so impressed by his genuine interest in the great man that he gave Dermot a gift of an old Calor gas stove and a medical journal that the explorer had apparently been using to look up his own symptoms just before his death. Uncertain as to whether he should accept the gifts Dermot decided instead to donate them to the museum – and found out that if he had sold them at auction he could have collected a suitably cool £60,000.

Next in Dermot's list of heroes is Shackleton's fellow explorer Tom Crean. 'He was as close to indestructible as a human being can be,' says Dermot. And indestructibility seems to be something Dermot admires. His key fictional hero is Indiana Jones – as a lifelong fan of Steven Spielberg films he says he was ready to break his abiding aversion to celebrity-studded red carpets and go to the latest premiere in 2008 just so he could see it a few days before everyone else.

Others he admires include the larger-than-life Irish actor Richard Harris and the late, former Northern Ireland secretary Mo Mowlam. The latter ticked several boxes in Dermot's mind. While her body had been weak, her spirit had certainly seemed indestructible and he admired the gutsy way she fought prejudice and illness alike. He also admits to being a far more politically aware man than most reality television fans may have thought. Yes, his picture might be in many of the tabloids and in most issues of *Heat* magazine. But his own reading matter is a very different matter.

He has a subscription to *National Geographic* magazine and is a regular reader of *Prospect* – a digest of heavy political essays and comment. And if that doesn't sound serious enough, the best issue Dermot has read in recent years was the one that was entirely devoted to the history, works and future of the United Nations. 'I took it on holiday and Dee was looking at me like I'm some kind of weirdo.'

While he needs to read the *Sun* to stay ahead of the light entertainment game, he admits he gets more out of the

Guardian and the *Independent*. Equally important to Dermot are his books on Irish politics and history. They were a way for him to reconnect with the country and the heritage he had felt adrift from as a boy and had moved even further from as a London-based television star. In truth, Ireland was rarely far from his mind. He says New York is his favourite non-Irish city in the world after London – and that was largely due to its huge Irish population and vast array of Irish bars and festivals. Seeing the headed notepaper of his production company Murfia also gave him a good feeling, as did a simple twist of the Claddagh ring his mum gave him when he was growing up and which is now one of his most treasured possessions. 'My link to Ireland has always been very important to me and I prefer to be known as Irish rather than English. I might not sound very Irish but cut me open and I bleed green Irish blood,' he once proclaimed.

And he always had a good welcome whenever he went 'home' or had any official dealings with the country. One thing he had vowed never to give up was his Irish passport. But he got a surprise when he had it renewed. Instead of his real name, Sean Dermot Finton O'Leary, he was listed as simple Dermot O'Leary. 'The girls in the Irish embassy knew who I was so they just automatically put Dermot on it,' he says. And while he doesn't know exactly why, that story kept him smiling for days.

In the summer of 2003, the smiles kept on coming. Because, at least for a while, Dermot's career was on a roll. This was the year that the *Big Brother* world hit an unexpected crisis – and Dermot was the only one to escape unscathed. The problem began with the year's housemates and developed with the tasks they were given to perform. Nothing sparked. The show was widely dubbed 'The Big Bore' and not even Davina could whip up much enthusiasm for the machinations or the weekly evictions.

But while ratings on the main show dipped, *BBLB* seemed to thrive. Dermot's freedom and freewheeling allowed him to go beyond doing a simple reportage job of the increasingly flat daily events. His lateral thinking gave him a chance to inject the humour and the interest that the housemates so desperately lacked. It meant that *BBLB* was more popular in 2003, not less. Some said that the future of the whole *Big Brother* bandwagon was in doubt that year. But Dermot sailed through it all.

Better still, he was justified in taking a big slice of the credit for keeping the magic alive. By 2003 he was *BBLB*'s associate producer as well as its presenter. He also wrote ever-growing sections of his script and that of many of the guests. That meant he needed to have a very clear idea of what he should and shouldn't do on screen. 'Like any little brother we can be mischievous,' was how he had famously put it when he launched the first series of his show. 'We love *Big Brother* but we're not averse to kicking our big brother in the shins and running away. We can have a slightly sideways glance at stuff.' In 2003, he was ready deliver in spades when this sense of mischief and the sideways glances were needed most of all.

No wonder, then, that Dermot ended 2003 on a high. One paper had actually captioned a photo of him with the words: 'The man who saved *Big Brother*' in a feature on the show's dull fourth year. Behind-the-scenes talk in production companies across the capital said the same.

Or at least it did in most production companies.

As he approached his fifth year as an on-screen presenter and had just scored his biggest professional triumph Dermot was starting to hear a few dissenting voices.

'Dermot is affable and engaged but he has to prove that he's not just a one-trick pony. This association with *Big Brother* is fine, but he has to perform beyond that niche. If he is not more adroit, he'll just get labelled a piece-to-camera monkey. It is very easy to be pigeonholed in this industry and Dermot is in danger of falling right into that trap'.

Ponies, monkeys, pigeonholes? When Dermot was told what one anonymous commissioning editor was reported to be saying about him he could have blown his top. He could have tracked down the speaker's name, called her up and demanded an apology.

But that, of course, was not his style.

From his childhood days watching Terry Wogan at the Shepherd's Bush Theatre, though his university days in Middlesex and his first few years behind the scenes in television, Dermot has proved one key thing: that he is never too proud to learn from the experts. He doesn't take criticism well. But if it is constructive then he will take it on board.

It meant that his high-powered critic got a fair hearing. Dermot agreed with some of her message. He was the first to admit that he too feared he had become pigeonholed – even though it was tough. 'For the past three years it seems as if the only shows that are getting made by the channels that I work with are reality shows. But I don't want to be Mr Reality.'

So why on earth did he agree to be the host of *Shattered*? This show had the potential to undo all his good work to date. For a moment it looked to be career-ending.

CHAPTER 11
CHOICES

It had seemed like a great idea at the time. As Dermot happily admits, reality shows were still all the rage. Producers were always having to raise the bar to get viewers interested. And at first *Shattered* certainly made the news.

The premise was very simple and very controversial. Keep people awake for up to seven days and see what happens. If *Big Brother* housemates were human guinea pigs in a social experiment then the *Shattered* contestants were human lab rats. And the moment news of the show leaked out, a host of experts came forward to say the experimentation could be dangerous. 'It's bad enough playing with people's minds. Playing with their health was a step too far,' said one. 'We may well have an insatiable appetite for trash TV but this doesn't mean the producers don't have a responsibility to their viewers as well as their contestants. Making fools of people is one thing. Putting them in danger is quite another. Everyone concerned with this show should be ashamed of themselves and consider their positions before we hit a new low for British broadcasting.'

Unfortunately Dermot was fully committed to the show by the time the media storm broke. He had signed his contract and couldn't back out. And neither could anyone else. The show was designed to fill an awful lot of hours on both Channel 4 and the still relatively new E4. A whole new set had been built to house it, deep inside the dark, mostly derelict Tobacco Dock in Wapping, East London. That was where the 12 contestants would live for up to seven days – competing for a £100,000 jackpot and, as usual, a slice of fame.

Dermot had agreed to live alongside them, though he would at least get to sleep. The producers had built him a little on-set bedroom where they placed a 'Dermot-Cam' above the bed to broadcast every rustle of the duvet live on the net. 'At least no one can say I don't suffer for my art,' Dermot joked to pals about the prospect of giving up his privacy for seven long nights. He laughed that he might lose a large slice of his fan base when he appeared on screen in his glasses, rather than his contacts. 'It will be the first time people realise you are short-sighted as well as short,' a friend told him with a smile.

But jokes apart, Dermot was stung by the criticism of the show – and of his role in hosting it. At first he tried to defend it, emphasising the fact that it wasn't quite as grim as the worst of the critics were making out. Yes, people did stupid things when they were dog tired so the show did promise some simple, slapstick entertainment. But it was also a relatively serious examination of human behaviour. Plenty of medical and psychological staff would be on hand to nip any potential problems in the bud. And, most fundamentally, watching people act when they are tired was surely safer than watching them when they are drunk, which was what a host of other fly-on-the-wall and reality shows set in holiday resorts seemed to be doing that year.

Having said his piece and made his excuses, Dermot turned up for work. He vowed to make the show a success and prove he had been right to take it on.

But he struggled. Introducing the contestants and setting the scene didn't have the buzz of a *Big Brother* launch night. The fact that it would all be over in a week took away much of the drama. And try as he might, Dermot didn't find it easy to get viewers interested in the participants themselves.

So in the end *Shattered* pretty much sank without trace. There had been tension, but beyond a few flash points there had been no real aggression. No one did get ill or harm themselves. It certainly hadn't been the end of civilisation as we know it. Few people can remember the name of the winner now, nor, really, what the point of the programme had been. And it wasn't even as if the Dermot-Cam had really revealed anything his fans had hoped to see.

Had it been worth it? Or had it been one reality show too far?

As usual, Dermot focused on the positive as he read some of the newspaper coverage and watched the tapes afterwards. He still reckons every minute he spends on screen is useful if it hones his skills and means that he can be an even more effective presenter in the future. And as he told *Sunday Telegraph* reporter Paul Morley, he had a few surprises in mind when asked what that future might hold.

PRESENTING DERMOT O'LEARY

'I am ambitious. But not with a capital A,' is how Paul remembers Dermot trying to explain it when they met. In theory the purpose of the interview had been to talk about Dermot's next job, taking over from Jamie Theakston and hosting Channel 4's *UK Music Hall of Fame*. 'Very quickly he slid off the topic and started to worry about the trajectory of his overall career and the frivolity of his profession,' Morley remembers. Being on *Hall of Fame* was great news, because it introduced Dermot to a newer, music focused audience. This was something he would soon consolidate by returning to his radio roots and building a reputation as a champion of new bands and live music on Radio Two. But in 2004 music wasn't the most important thing on Dermot's mind. He was more concerned about his choice of television roles. 'Yes, I worry that *Big Brother's Little Brother* might have cost me the more, shall we say, cerebral jobs, even at Channel 4,' he said. Morley remembers thinking that the way Dermot joked about missing out on the presenter's role for More 4's new topical discussion show *The Last Word* were a little too forced. It seemed that Dermot did care that he had been barely considered for the job.

'This is not just some youth television lightweight,' Morley thought to himself. 'It is obvious that he is a man on a mission. On the quiet he wants to establish himself as a television great, a broadcasting legend'. Now, this might sound ridiculously over the top – but Dermot then confirmed it. 'Presenting can be physically and mentally intensive but really it's an easy job and you are paid a disproportionate amount of money,' Dermot admitted. 'At the moment I am a presenter, not a broadcaster. A broadcaster is more substantial. I'm not there yet,' Dermot had said, a distant look in his eyes.

What Morley and many others in the industry were starting to realise was that Dermot intended to get there. He would have worked on almost any show going at the start of his career simply to get his foot in the door and earn the experience he knew he needed. After *Shattered* he vowed to be more discerning. He suddenly realised that he was no longer bothered by ratings. What he wanted was respect.

For Dermot respect is very real. It is not something that is demanded, nor is it the juvenile, debased respect of teenage street gangs. For Dermot, respect is something that has to be earned. And it is something that can only be handed out by those you respect in return. In his case by his peers in the industry he loved. But how to earn it? And what to do next?

As Dermot's new approach gathered steam, he knew that he could at least rely on a very impressive contact list and some very powerful friends. In the autumn of 2004 he was spotted in some stellar restaurants having lunch with some very influential people. One day he was seen with Lorraine Heggessey, then controller of BBC One. Another he was deep in conversation with Kevin Lygo, Channel 4's director of television. Television insiders put an interesting spin on what was going on. 'It's all positive except that no one knows exactly what to do with him. Dermot's CV is eclectic but it conveys the impression of someone in need of the right gig,' said TV expert Harriet Lane, who interviewed Dermot for the *Observer* that autumn.

Dermot confirmed her thoughts. 'The schtick I'm getting from programmers at the moment is that they want me on their channel but they're not entirely sure where. They like me, they just don't know where to put me, which is a weird situation.'

While the various broadcasters tried to make up their minds Channel 4 came up with a fun stop-gap solution. The bosses there knew he was a perfect 'face' for their channel. That's why he was lined up alongside the likes of Gordon Ramsay, *ER* star Parminder Nagra and *Desperate Housewives* actress Felicity Huffman for a new series of the iconic 'idents' for the channel – the little clips that appear between programmes to remind us which channel we're watching. Dermot's best was the one where everyone described their first car and he got the longer slot at the end where he hammed up a scenario suggesting his was being vandalised just off camera. Others included him giving his favourite inventions and foods. The cameos were filmed in half a dozen different locations around London and only took a matter of hours to complete. Dermot had the same crew for many of them and enjoyed himself. But when the filming was over all the old insecurities came back.

'Some days you feel you are at the top of the world and that everyone wants to work with you and other days you sit at home and you think, "What am I doing wrong?" and you wonder if you can ever get the kinds of jobs you really want,' he admitted. Buzzing over it all was his now constant desire to get the message across that there was more to Dermot O'Leary than cheesy reality TV. '*BB* is the only reality show I do,' he told people now that *Shattered* was over. 'And *BBLB* isn't reality TV at all. It's an entertainment and news show that happens to be based around people who all live in a house.'

A fresh-faced Dermot pictured in 1999, shortly after getting his big break on *T4*.

Above: With *Top of the Pops* presenters Jamie Theakston and Zoe Ball. Dermot was a guest presenter on the famous BBC show.

© *Nils Jorgensen/Rex Features*

Below: A typical Irish lad! Dermot enjoys a pint of Guinness in a pub near his home in North London.

© *Rex Features*

Above left: As his profile has risen, so Dermot has had to get used to being in the glare of the press.

© *Brian Rasic/Rex Features*

Above right: Dermot outside the 2003 *Big Brother* house. He loved the chance to go behind the scenes on the show.

© *Rex Features*

Below: Dermot is always keen to help young people get into the TV industry – here he's pictured in Belfast at an event helping the stars of the future learn TV skills.

© *Mirrorpix*

Above left: Dermot with his beloved Mum.
© *Julian Makey/Rex Features*

Above right: Dermot and long-term girlfriend Dee. The pair like to keep out of the public eye as much as possible, and have so far succeeded in keeping their relationship private.
© *Mr. JCY/Rex Features*

Left: Dermot combining his love of sport with his interest in charity work, taking part in a Sport Relief charity cricket match in Mumbai.
© *Ben Radford/Getty Images*

Raising money and awareness for charity means a lot to Dermot.

Above: Supporting the Everyman campaign to raise awareness of male cancer.

© *Ferdus Shamim/WireImage/Getty Images*

Below left: Squeezing into Gareth Gates's white suit at the Crusaid charity auction in 2002 – Dermot ended up with the winning bid, buying the suit for £15,000! © *Ken McKay/Rex Features*

Below right: Running the London Marathon in 2003. Dermot has taken part in several charity marathons and half-marathons, clocking in at under four hours for the first time in 2005.

© *Stephen Butler/Rex Features*

Above: Taking part in the UK Radio Aid 12-hour broadcast marathon in 2005, to raise money for victims of the Asian tsunami. Dermot presented the first of the shows, from 6am to 8am, with *Big Brother* chum Davina McCall.

© *Ian West/PA Photos*

Below: *Big Brother* was one of Dermot's most successful programmes, winning the National Television Awards gong for Most Popular Reality Programme in 2005 and 2006.

© *Nils Jorgensen/Rex Features; Ray Tang/Rex Features*

Above: One of the most challenging moments of Dermot's career to date – interviewing Jade Goody after her exit from the *Celebrity Big Brother* house amid a storm over alleged racist comments.

© *Rex Features*

Below left: Dermot's first series of *X Factor* was a dramatic one, with Leon Jackson (right) scooping first prize ahead of favourite Rhydian Roberts (left).

© *Nils Jorgensen/Rex Features; Ray Tang/Rex Features*

Below right: *X Factor* has brought Dermot more awards success – here he is pictured with *X Factor* judges Louis Walsh, Sharon Osbourne, Simon Cowell and Dannii Minogue at the National Television Awards in 2007.

© *Dave M Benett/Getty Images*

Dermot's career is going
from strength to strength and
with another massive series
of *X Factor* in 2010, he's sure
to be on our screens for
many years to come.

CHOICES

What Dermot needed was to choose a show that would at once be very genuine, very unique and very personal. That, and that alone, could resuscitate his career and lift him to a new level. And one day he woke up and realised he knew exactly what the show should be about. It was something that had been part of him all his life. It was his religion.

In his early days as Prime Minister, Tony Blair famously said that the British 'don't do God'. His feeling was that we are all a little embarrassed about public displays of religious belief. But Dermot wasn't embarrassed. Even as a child he had been proud to be an altar boy. He had never felt ashamed of the clothes and the rituals of the church – in fact he had positively thrived upon them. At Catholic school he had continued to enjoy his spiritual journey. As an adult, his faith had guided him away from some of the pitfalls of modern life. So as a public figure he felt he had an obligation to use his profile and his position to explain some of his deeper thoughts.

He first stepped out of his youth television bubble into the complex world of religious argument when he was asked to contribute to an anthology of essays entitled 'Why I am Still a Catholic', put together by the author and theologian Peter Stanford. From the start Dermot was in very good company indeed. Baroness Scotland and Monsignor Bruce Kent were among his co-writers. But Dermot's contribution, about the 'pick 'n' mix' approach to faith that had been dubbed 'cafeteria Catholicism', got some of the best reviews.

When the anthology was reviewed in the *Daily Telegraph*, the paper's religious correspondent began by saying that

Dermot O'Leary's inclusion in the book might puzzle some older readers. But the writer said it shouldn't put them off. 'In fact O'Leary's is in some ways the most interesting piece in the book because he is not afraid to articulate the position of the cafeteria Catholic,' said the *Telegraph*'s commentary. Here are some of Dermot's words.

> Yes, I go to Mass and am a regular communicant. Yes, I hate abortion and see it for what it is, though I accept that it exists. But I use contraception. I'm not married to my girlfriend. I have gay friends. And I don't believe, as the Creed puts it, that there is only one baptism for the forgiveness of sins.

It was bravely and cleverly written – a light and personal way to cover profound and difficult issues. And as time went on Dermot found he wanted to speak out on the subject again. But he would never be some very polite Cliff Richard style of commentator. 'The Pope's a great man. He's done a lot of great things. But he's also made a lot of dumbass moves,' was one of his typically forthright comments on the subject.

Now, with his career in a state of flux, he turned back to religion to give him the credibility he craved.

Forget his old comfort zone and the constant offers of new reality shows to present. Instead he signed up to work on the documentary *Some Of My Best Friends Are ... Catholic*. The show was one of four programmes in which different hosts examined the state of their religion today and their own positions within the faiths. In the other three half-hour programmes the journalist and author Yasmin Alibhai-Brown examined Islam, the writer and broadcaster Rod Liddle looked at the Church of England, and Anita Land covered the Jewish religion. In his show – broadcast in a prime 7.30pm slot – Dermot spoke to trainee priests, modern monks and everybody in between. He took soundings on the way the Catholic faith had changed in the past and might change again in the future. And he asked tough questions about the way his own life meshed into the key beliefs. It was profound, slow-paced and as far from *T4* and *The Dog's Balearics* as it is possible to be. But Dermot, after a few teething troubles, was in his element. From the start he was entirely committed to making the programme a success – even if it gave him sleepless nights in the process.

The man who describes himself as 'surprisingly and increasingly introspective' says, 'I would finish each day's work on that show and my brain wouldn't stop churning. I had a headache all the way through.'

One interesting aside is that for Dermot recorded television proved more stressful than live TV. When you aren't able to change things or do re-takes you live on your adrenaline and sink or swim in the moment. When you have plenty of time to make the perfect programme you dwell on each scene and worry constantly about whether you should try it one more time to see if it can be improved. When the final deadlines came and the editing was done Dermot got a far greater sense of relief than on any of his more manic live shows. This short, one-off, low-audience show had really meant something to him. But would his message get lost in translation?

Some critics said Dermot was out of his depth on the show. In some respects Dermot agreed with them – this was his first entirely self-penned documentary after all. But for once he wouldn't have cared if all the reviews had been bad. This wasn't *Shattered*. It wasn't a programme he would ever regret, not least because it had given him the chance to confirm his own thoughts about his faith. 'In purely selfish terms it was worth the anxiety because it reaffirmed what I think, what I believe,' he said. 'I met some great men, religious men, who said that you have to question faith. That you can't follow scripture verbatim. You've got to use it as a guide.'

In the end, Dermot felt it had been brilliant to take such a personal journey – and to try and take the viewers along with him. And the programmed did indeed take his career on to that vital new level. The following year Dermot was told that this, his first serious, 'grown-up' show, had won him his first broadcasting award, The Sandford St Martin Trust Religious Broadcasting Award for 2004. It was a personal triumph. His family, in Essex and in County Wexford, were hugely proud of him. And it was a vital professional honour as well. Dermot's peers in the broadcasting industry were suddenly aware that the smiling Essex boy with the Irish name could do more than front pop and reality shows. What he had achieved had been duly noted. It was clear that the programme, and the award, could open important doors for the youngster in the future.

'What television needs is credibility,' says broadcasting commentator and media studies lecturer Russell Drake. 'With luck, the days are passing when unsuitable people are parachuted into ill-fitting shows simply to chase ratings or fulfil contractual obligations. What the industry needs is for the right people to be put in the right roles. Dermot is probably too young to be offered or even to want some sort of religious broadcasting show. But *Some Of My Best Friends* proved that he could be a contender for more serious, factual programmes. That will give him plenty of options for the future.'

Even better news for Dermot after *Some Of My Best Friends* was that unlike many presenters he no longer needed to sit around waiting for the right jobs to come to him. He had the power to create them from scratch. His production company Murfia was now in full swing, discussing and devising a near-endless set of possible shows for Dermot and his colleagues. One early effort was a pilot for *The Parent Trap*, which took a clever new look at the old chestnut of the generation gap. BBC Three bought it and a six-part series went on air, giving Dermot a nice slice of money and even more artistic credibility.

But he did admit that the sales process for *The Parent Trap* hadn't been easy. He both loved and hated the role of company boss. It was exciting and empowering. But it was also worryingly stressful and he ended up feeling surprisingly vulnerable. When he had just been the on-screen talent backing up other people's production ideas he had been shielded from the brutality of the broadcasting industry. Now that he was the one trying to pitch the ideas themselves the knock-backs felt a little harder.

Having business partners and employees, albeit freelance ones, also added a new layer of responsibility.

Dermot hated letting people down. He could handle his own disappointments, but he didn't enjoy inflicting them on others.

That's one reason why he barely thought twice when he agreed to re-sign for another long-term job. No, it wasn't something that would build upon the serious success of his award-winning documentary. No, it wasn't something that would be totally unique and allow him to stamp his own identity on a brand new show. No, it wasn't necessarily going to stretch him very much or teach him any new broadcasting skills. But, heck, it had always been a vast amount of fun. And in 2005 – after a three-year gap – *Celebrity Big Brother* was coming back.

CHAPTER 12

CELEBRITIES – AND HOUSEMATES

The first *Celebrity Big Brother* in 2001 had been an experiment – not least because much of the show was broadcast on the BBC rather than Channel 4. The show had been set up as a rare collaboration between the two channels and was designed as a one-off way to raise extra cash for Comic Relief. Six celebrities, Chris Eubank, Anthea Turner, Keith Duffy, Vanessa Feltz, Claire Sweeney and Jack Dee all entered the house for up to eight days.

As media-aware performers none were expected to behave particularly badly. None were expected to be phased by the cameras or bothered by the directions from *Big Brother*. But that's when the fun began. Almost all the housemates defied expectations by behaving bizarrely – Vanessa most famously of all. And it pushed ratings through the roof. The show was far more popular than the producer's secret (but leaked) projections. And the media interest was intense. Newspapers and celebrity magazines couldn't get enough of the celebrities. So after attempted escapee Jack Dee was declared the winner there were already plans for a second version in 2002. That year Anne Diamond made most of the headlines and Mark Owen was declared the winner.

After a three-year gap the public – and Dermot – were very ready for a third outing in 2005. And everyone wanted the celebrities to behave even worse than ever. They didn't disappoint – though with the likes of Germaine Greer, Jackie Stallone, Brigitte Nielsen and John McCririck in the mix they were never really going to go quietly. One of Dermot's early fears about *CBB* was that it might take attention away from the flagship summer show. He feared it might cannibalise the brand and kill the goose that had laid so many golden eggs. He was happy to admit he was wrong. The new show seemed only to increase our passion for the whole *Big Brother* concept. So Dermot's year would continue to be dominated by events in the various houses – celebrities in the spring, the public in the summer. It was a brilliant opportunity. Branching out into other areas would have to wait a while.

The only fly in the ointment as 2005 turned to 2006 was a slight worry that Dermot's good nature and enthusiasm for *Big Brother* had been exploited by the producers. Industry insiders said Davina was likely to be earning £550,000 for each series of the summer show, plus an extra £250,000 for the celebrity version. Those same industry insiders put Dermot on 'just' £10,000 a week for both productions. 'Davina is good at her job but she is paid a fortune for it. Dermot is a professional, but it must rankle that he is doing more than twice the work for considerably less money,' one anonymous producer told *Daily Mirror* reporters when the pay gap was first revealed. And it was a problem. Dermot readily accepts that he was collecting far more than most people dream of earning. He feels appallingly guilty when he thinks of nurses and police officers and other low-paid staff working unsocial hours for a fraction of his total rewards. But he knew that there was a principal at stake. He knew that employers shouldn't be allowed to take advantage of anyone's guilt or good will. He made a push for a fair wage – just as Davina kindly admitted that there was a clear gap in their respective work loads. 'He's there every day and I waft in on a Friday. Work-wise all I have to do is what I would be doing every day as a viewer because I would be watching it every day,' she admitted.

For Dermot, coming up with fresh guests, fresh concepts and fresh treatments for each daily show, the pressure was far more intense. Dermot's problems were compounded by the fact that he couldn't follow Davina's lead and build his shows around the big set-piece events like the weekly evictions. He had to hold his viewers' attentions throughout some long, difficult shows. So it was just as well he was getting increasingly good at choosing his guests.

Over the years Dermot has become something of a star-maker. Mathew Horne was a guest back when he was only just becoming known on the *Catherine Tate Show*. He and Dermot hit it off from the start and stayed in touch off screen. Now they are firm friends – which is a rare honour for Dermot who continues to shun new, high-profile mates and spends most of his time with Dee and their long-term pals. In 2007, when Mathew ended up hosting *Big Brother's Big Mouth* with his *Gavin and Stacey* co-star James Corden, no one was more pleased than Dermot. But if Mathew and James could get these kinds of promotion, couldn't Dermot?

For a while it was hard to ignore the rumours that Dermot was going to replace Davina on the flagship *Big Brother* show. But she certainly didn't look ready to leave. 'Are you ready to hand over the presenting torch to someone else and leave *Big Brother*?' she was asked as long ago as 2005. 'They would have to cut off my right arm and prise the torch forcefully from my hand,' was her very famous reply. Dermot had to take that as a 'no'. And he kept on saying that he was happy with the status quo. 'I don't want her job. I have far more fun doing my job than she does doing hers,' he said, inadvertently setting off a whole new set of rumours that an unhappy Davina might be on the point of quitting.

But amid all the rumours about presenters and their musical chairs one truth stood out. Back then Dermot still genuinely loved the show. '*Big Brother* takes over my life,' he joked. 'I'm so sad that I sit on the sofa at home, watch all the housemates go to bed, wait until they go to sleep then spend half-an-hour watching them sleeping before I go to bed myself.' Even then it wasn't over. Dermot says most nights he dreams about the housemates as well. He has never gone into that many details about these fantasies. But he admits that some of the situations might make even a psychiatrist blush.

Back in the cleverly constructed madhouse of *BBLB* the good guests kept on coming. Dermot and his team were able to call up everyone who is anyone – and Dermot got to meet an awful lot of his life-long heroes and heroines. Two favourites included Kathy Burke (who he still raves about to this day) and Bob Mortimer (whose comments still make him laugh when he replays the tapes).

But when you are doing a daily show for months at a time, then it is really only a numbers game until some bad apples tumble out of the bag. He admits that basketball star Dennis Rodman was a particular challenge. 'He was an idiot,' Dermot has been widely quoted as saying (perhaps bravely, considering the large height and weight difference between the pair of them). What made it even worse was that Dermot had been a basketball fan ever since he'd started playing American football back in Colchester. He had admired Dennis Rodman as a player and had been equally fascinated by his colourful personal life. 'I had really been looking forward to interviewing him,' Dermot says. But the big man wasn't really up for it. He'd been in a lap-dancing club most of the previous night, Dermot later found out. He swore a lot before the cameras clicked on. And neither his mood nor his language improved very much once the broadcast began.

The all-time Dermot O'Leary Award for Show's Worst Guest goes to glamour girl Alicia Duvall. Many said she could be a contender for the title of worst guest in the history of television full stop. And that includes Meg Ryan's morose, monosyllabic performance on Parkinson in 2003, Grace Jones battering Russell Harty in 1981 and Joan Collins, David Bowie and George Best all producing memorably bad moments on *Wogan*.

Dermot says he knew that things were going to go wrong with Alicia the moment she got to the *BBLB* set. Her body language told him that she wasn't ready to play any games. And within seconds of the live interview beginning he knew it was shot to pieces. But when you have many minutes to fill and nothing else to fall back on there is precious little you can do but carry on regardless. So Dermot kept trying to get some sense out of his guest. He deserved a medal. 'She was unspeakably bad,' he says now when he thinks back to the interview. 'But it was one of my favourite episodes. Years later people still ask me about that interview – and yes I would have her back on the show in a heartbeat. I'd love to try that again,' he says with a huge smile.

Of the housemates Dermot has also had his clear favourites – and a fair share of those he hopes he will never see again. Just like Davina, he says that during a show's run he is forced to be diplomatic and 'isn't allowed' to have favourites. But afterwards? That's a different matter. Then it's open season.

Two names crop up when he is asked about the sexiest housemates – and one of them is normally a surprise. The first is Shell Jubin from *Big Brother 5* in 2004 who Dermot places as the sexiest ever – so sexy he reckoned even Dee fancied her, though he later said this spoke more about his own sexual feelings than those of his girlfriend. The second name came up last year. 'Of all the *Big Brother* contestants who would you sleep with?' he was asked by a group of journalism students. With a characteristically cheeky grin he picked transsexual Nadia Almada. 'Just for the hell of it' was his reason. His fans, gay or straight, male, female or anything in between, all seemed to love it.

Sex appeal apart, what grips Dermot most about the shows are the housemates who go on the longest personal journeys in the house. Model turned author Aisleyne Horgan-Wallace from *Big Brother 7* in 2006, who entered the house late, fought back against the bullies and ended the year as the best-ranked female in the house, is a key example. 'It's incredible to watch people learn more about themselves as the weeks go by,' he says. 'It's particularly moving when people learn that they are better than they had thought or can do more than they had realised. The best of *Big Brother* can empower people. It can give them the strength and confidence to be who they really are and change their lives for the better.'

What Dermot has also enjoyed most is the psychology of the show. His eyes have always focused on the side stories that developed while most others were looking at the main event. When Jade did her infamous drunken strip in 2002 Dermot did, of course, sneak a peak as her 'kebab belly' went on display and she ran naked to the bedroom. But more interesting to his mind was the look of amazement and horror on fellow housemate Kate Lawler's face as the storyline played itself out. He had been fascinated by the dynamics between the two competing women in the final stages of that year's show. He loved trying to decide if sisterly solidarity would triumph over their joint desires to win the show. He likes trying to see if any housemate, any year, has learned the lessons from the past or is about to make all the same mistakes again.

His conclusion in all this is that the women are the ones who play the game the best – just as he thinks they do in the world at large. In almost every respect, Dermot feels that if there were to be a sex war his money would go on the women. 'The women play the game in a much smarter way,' he told

Observer reporter Rebecca Seal. 'I'm not suggesting that these women use their bodies for the *Big Brother* game, but they're definitely in charge. I don't mean in a sexual way – it has more to do with influence and power. I remember even when I was five, growing up in Colchester, if a girl in the playground even looked at me twice I walked on air all week. It's that sort of power that women have over men. It's generally thought that women are emotional and men aren't. But I think it's the other way around. When men go, they really go and there's no retrieving them. Even on a day-to-day basis, all the women in my life have always just sat down in a crisis and said, right, this is what's happened and this is what we are going to do about it. Us men just lose it.'

Of the female *Big Brother* housemates he reckons Makosi Musambasi from series six was one of the best at these sexual power games. But when it comes to using sexual wiles for pure entertainment value he says Nikki Grahame has to claim the prize. 'What didn't I enjoy about Nikki?' he laughed. 'She does come with some baggage but she's an extraordinary character – the tantrums are unbelievable.' He also said that Nikki's shock early eviction in 2006 was proof that *BB* was sound, despite a spate of television-voting scandals on other programmes. 'If they could fix it I am sure that the programme makers would have moved heaven and earth to keep her in there, so her eviction showed there's no way the show can be fixed.' And, oh boy, did he have fun interviewing the mad princess when Nikki finally made her noisy, tear-stained and unmissable entry into the *BBLB* studio.

A final glimpse of the secret feminist in Dermot came in

2007 when a *Times* reader took a light-hearted pot shot at Amanda and Sam Marchant, the twins who entered *Big Brother 8* together. The joke came in the paper's 'air bubble caption' competition – it prints a topical picture with a blank bubble coming out of the subject's head and asks readers to suggest thoughts to put in it for the following week. When it came to the twins, the winning entry was from a reader who had left the thought bubbles entirely empty. But Dermot had already spotted that the twins were far from empty-headed idiots. He had a feeling they would prove a lot cleverer than they looked. Less than a year later, when their combined earnings were estimated to have approached the £1 million mark, he was proved right.

Of the blokes, Dermot's favourites have been a lot more low-key – and a little less predictable. He particularly liked Jon Tickle from *Big Brother 4* in 2003. Jon was one of the very few housemates he has kept in touch with over the years, though their get-togethers are few and far between. So why Jon? One reason is that he was so different to all the other fame-seeking housemates. Jon entered the house a nice, ordinary guy, left the house a nice, ordinary guy and by all accounts has remained one ever since. He played the fame game after leaving the house the way everyone did – and in many ways he has been more successful than most. But when his 15 minutes of crazy fame appeared to be up he was ready to accept it with good grace. That's how he earned Dermot's respect and friendship.

What Dermot doesn't want are housemates who cling to him in order to stay in the public eye – or ones who see him as offering a way into a world he isn't even a part of. 'The one thing they all want to do when they come out is to go to Chinawhite and all these parties, and those kinds of things aren't really my bag,' says the coolest old-fogey on telly.

That said, Dermot's innate sense of fair play does sometimes get the better of him as the housemates join him on the *BBLB* sofa. He has a complex mix of sympathy for, and wariness of, the housemates. And he has always said that while he happily takes the mickey out of them he will never be gratuitously cruel. 'By the time I meet them, if they haven't behaved well then they have already been vilified. So it would be like shooting a wounded puppy if I was too tough on them,' is how he sees it. And that's not all. He knows, better than most, how the modern media works. So he does feel a certain allegiance for the people he has been watching almost 24 hours a day. 'Yes, I do feel I have to look out for them sometimes, otherwise they'll sign up with all these dodgy agents. Every now and then I'll give my number to the ones I like. I'll say "Look, it's going to be quite hairy for you soon", but there's a limit to how much anyone can warn them about the way the media may treat them and the way their lives may change.'

But back to the fun housemates and the good times.

Dermot says he totally 'got' series two winner Brian Dowling and knew that the former air steward would win the show in the first week. He says that one of his all-time favourite moments was of Alex Sibley singing behind the bathroom door *Big Brother 3*.

But his other favourites are something of a surprise. And as the first person after Davina to interview them – and the first to ask them to do more than answer questions – Dermot knows he gets a unique window into their worlds. As he tends to have them back on the show night after night in their first post-eviction week, he says he can also track how they deal with sudden celebrity. That too can be a surprise.

'Often the people you think you're going to dislike turn out to be okay and vice versa. Science was horrible when he was in the house – he was really nasty to a lot of people. And then he came out and I've never met a more polite, well-raised, humble man,' he says. Science also passed the 'sudden celebrity' test. Dermot says he stayed the same good character throughout his week on *BBLB*. 'He didn't change, which some of them do.' Among the blokes, other perhaps surprising favourites include Victor Ebuwa from *BB5* who Dermot thought was treated horribly by the press, and the dashing Derek Laud from *BB6* the following year.

Dermot also enjoys telling friends of the bizarre behind-the-scenes stories of *BBLB* itself. When Ahmed Aghil was in the house in 2004 there was this one weird scene when, under pressure to nominate a housemate for eviction, he had yelled out: 'I am not a sandwich!' – creating a mini catchphrase for the summer. 'For the little pre-titles teaser at the start of the show we decided to build this huge foam sandwich and get Ahmed to lie on it so he could say, "I've changed my mind. I am a sandwich." Which we all thought would be funny. Anyway, it was all going well and he was lying there during rehearsals when he said to the props girl, "What's this red stuff?" underneath him. She said: "Oh, I dunno, bacon maybe?" And he said: "I won't lie in bacon. I'm a Muslim." So she said: "Okay then, it's tomato." But he was having none of it. "No, no, you said it was bacon," he's saying. And I'm standing there thinking, haven't they slightly missed the point – it was a piece of foam.'

So, as *Big Brother* and *BBLB* rolled on each and every summer, was there ever a moment when Dermot thought it had gone too far? Or that it had reached the end of its shelf life?

For a long time he would defend the show to the hilt – and he meant every word he said. When people attacked it as a freak show in the Jade era, when they said it was exploiting people with mental illnesses in the Pete Bennett year, when they said it encouraged bullying, let alone racially tinted bullying in the *Celebrity* years, he would always say the same thing. 'If you watch the show, if you really watch it, then you'll see it's fair to everyone – and that includes the viewers.'

He was equally angry at accusations that the producers – and by implication he and Davina – were exploiting vulnerable housemates. Simply not true, he said. 'Of all the reality shows I think *Big Brother* is also the most honest. That's what I like about it. People that are going into the house know exactly what to expect. They've got no complaints when they come out. They know they're going to have two weeks of notoriety and then it will tail off. And they will make a lot of money in those two weeks. Nine times out of ten I would say that people who have gone in the house say their lives have changed for the better, be it financially or otherwise, when they come out.'

Dermot was on equally strong form when it came to rumours that the show was tired and past its best. He admits he can see why people made the accusations. But he didn't agree with the common conclusions. 'We've had some big characters over the years and you really miss them and think you'll never get anyone as good again. Every single year I ask myself how long I think *Big Brother* will last, but as long as there is an appetite for it then it will keep going. We have good characters, good stories and some of the housemates go on a real journey. It's a kind of weird fairy tale every summer. And I like the fact that it still provokes debate. I like the fact that some people still slag it off and the fact that other people slag people for slagging it. It's great that it's that culturally important.'

And he had a good way to prove to himself that the show was hitting all its possible targets. One day he logged on at work and saw an email from zoologist and film-maker Desmond Morris. He turned out to be a fan – and saw the show as a perfect way to explore human interaction. Dermot had first heard about Desmond as a school boy when some of the 'racy' pictures in his books were passed around the playground by the older kids. In time, though, Dermot got to read the text that accompanied them and became a fan of the author's theories on social development. All those years on it felt great to think that the author now approved of *Big Brother* – especially because a mini-backlash seemed to be in the air.

'Who are the real *Big Brother* winners?' the papers started to ask in 2006 when a new wave of criticism against the show began to hit. Dermot and Davina were put forward as the real victors, having built long careers and earned big bucks out of everyone else's embarrassment. But Dermot in particular made no apologies for the fact that few of the housemates could ever hope to match the presenters' earning power or staying power. 'The contestants are told: "Look, if you want fame, go and audition for something like *Pop Idol* because you're not going to get it here. You'll make a bit of money and you'll come out and people will like you, and in equal measure people will hate you. We're not going to promise you anything more than that." And the contestants understand that. That's why there's nothing unfair about the show.'

Dermot was just as supportive of the show's staff and structure when attacks came from other quarters. He felt he had to be because he felt so close to the whole *Big Brother* family. Over the years he had turned into a lot more than just a fan and a presenter. He was a paid-up member of the gang. He played football with a team from the camera crew and loved the fact that so many of the same production team came back to the show year after year, series after series. Then, of course, came his bond with Davina. He said that right from the start the pair had got on 'like a house on fire'. He calls her 'D' (sometimes 'big D') gets on well with her three kids and says he wishes they lived closer so they could see even more of each other out of 'office' hours. He has also proved to be a loyal and vocal friend when the chips were down. In the spring of 2006 he defended her to the hilt over her ill-fated chat show on BBC One for example.

'A bad show doesn't mean a bad presenter. I think she was really badly treated over that,' he says. And he had given his pal's situation a great deal of thought, concluding that much of the criticism was misplaced misogyny. 'Hand on heart I don't think the vitriol would have been so bad if it had been a man,' he said. 'The TV industry is brutal to women. If I put on a couple of pounds I'm not going to lose a job. Nor if I get a couple of wrinkles. I could pretty much jump out of bed, get into a shower, and then wear minimal make-up and get away with it. A woman would get hauled up in a string of magazines if she did that. Sexism is inherent in TV. One of the major problems with telly today is that it doesn't breed many women to drive a show like Davina can. Instead it breeds men to do it, and women to either look good or to be the sidekick.'

Supporting Davina won Dermot some very good press. But things weren't so positive when another 'colleague' ended up in the media firing line the following year. This was the year of Shilpa-gate in Celebrity *Big Brother*, when Jade Goody made headlines around the world for her alleged racist comments. Jade, at that point, was being managed by the John Noel agency, which also represented Davina, Russell Brand and, crucially, Dermot.

When Jade left the house everyone was watching the interviews she gave to see how she responded to the criticism and indeed how harsh the criticism would be. Dermot tried to be both firm and fair in his far from comfortable interview. He felt he asked her what had to be asked and tried hard not to let her evade giving clear answers. It wasn't easy. And Dermot left the studio feeling distinctly unhappy. 'It was horrible. She needs anger management and therapy,' was all Dermot would say of the interviewee.

But at the time plenty of others had something to say

about it. Critics said Dermot let Jade off too lightly – that he allowed her to make too many excuses and avoid taking responsibility for her actions. They then came up with the conspiracy theory that Dermot (and indeed Davina) had been told to go easy on Jade to protect their agent's investment. Dermot and Davina have both consistently denied the allegations, and were soon off the hook when Jade parted company with John Noel and looked for new representation elsewhere.

Incidentally, Dermot has other strong opinions on the 2007 *Celebrity Big Brother* debacle. He has argued that the fights were more to do with class, education and age than with race. 'Basically you had Jade Goody, a street-smart girl from south London whose back was put up by a middle-class Indian woman,' is how he sees it. And he is particularly angry at the way politicians and the like weighed in to attack a show they didn't actually watch. 'I was furious at that. The critics were so grossly opinionated about the show, but it provoked a debate that MPs could only dream of doing.' He felt that the show should actually be praised for airing the whole subject of racism – and by proving that racist comments, real or imagined, will always be totally condemned.

By the end of each series of *Big Brother* – celebrity or otherwise – the adrenaline can sometimes run dry and the tensions can mount. Dermot is happy to admit that he can be both 'cranky and snappy' when he is hungry or tired – and that life behind the scenes isn't always pure sweetness and light. He admits to being a perfectionist and says he can snap at people when he feels things aren't going as well as they should. 'I think I'm low maintenance at work but I do get immensely angry – though at myself more than at other people,' he says.

Exhaustion often set in because the *BBLB* gig actually lasted a lot longer than the series itself. Dermot and his team were on set and in pre-production long before the housemates arrived. And they put in far more hours during each series than were ever broadcast. Some of this extra work was essential, energising and good fun. Dermot particularly liked his special access to the house – he loved wandering around looking through the two-way mirrors as the tasks were set up. He also liked seeing the secret footage that couldn't be broadcast for legal reasons.

In an admission that would prove very useful when he won the *X Factor* gig, Dermot also loved being able to review some of the audition footage, though before each series he never sat in on any of the interviews or discussed potential housemates with Endemol producers. What he did get to do was find out far earlier than the rest of us about any twists or tricks in that year's *Big Brother* narrative. Whether it was 'secret houses' or a late delivery of fresh housemates he loved being in the loop, though he always struggled to keep the producers' secrets.

At the end of each increasingly draining series Dermot did at least go out with a bang. He thrived on the chance to do the warm-up show for the housemates' friends and family before each final. It took him back to his first days in broadcasting with Mel and Sue on *Light Lunch*, and as he didn't present the final show himself, it signalled a chance for him to relax as the events of the final unfolded. 'After that I don't have to do anything. I can just sit on my arse, have a drink and enjoy it!' he joked. The following day, though, he always made a personal television pilgrimage. He used his staff pass and was allowed to sneak into the house itself – normally in carnage the morning after the night before.

He says he used to wander around in silence, trying to imagine just how hard it would have been to spend so long inside those shiny, reflective walls. The only thing he didn't do, having embarrassed himself in the past, is have a pee. 'You just never know if one lone camera might still be on,' he revealed. Then, one day after the last housemates are granted their freedom, he could finally relax. The crew have said that he was normally one of the most fun staffers at each year's wrap party for the series – a point that is easily proved if you look at some grainy mobile phone footage of him on YouTube. It's the night he took to the wrap party's makeshift stage to sing along to 'Karaoke Rock Star' in his now trademark shiny grey suit and thin black tie.

'A loveable geek,' was how one viewer described him. Another said the video proved why he would one day host the *X Factor* rather than appear on it as a contestant.

But while singing live might not have been a great career move for Dermot his commitment to the best new music certainly was. Because a few years earlier Dermot had gone back to his radio roots. Then he had agreed to take that career move to the next level. Radio Two might not exactly be the coolest station in the world, but it was where Dermot's original hero Terry Wogan had made his name. It was where his next professional role model, Jonathan Ross, had carved out a huge new fan base. Dermot wanted to muscle in on their turf. He was up for yet another professional challenge.

CHAPTER 13

THE MUSIC MAN

The nerdy little kid who had grown up liking ELO and big Bruce Springsteen numbers has come a heck of a long way. His school pals might not have always approved of his choices from the Britannia Music Club catalogues. But follow Dermot's musical journey and you see he has nothing to be ashamed of today.

Former colleagues say he still had the most mainstream of tastes back on local radio in Essex. But he began to change shortly after moving to London. That was when he decided to get to grips with the indie scene.

He got an opportunity to prove his interest from indie rock station Xfm, which had launched in London in 1997. Dermot scored a show there at a perfect time. It was 2001, when he had left *T4*, and as he was still in talks about the concept show that would become *BBLB* he was a little bit worried about paying the bills. A regular show on radio would take the pressure off while keeping his old skills from Essex up to scratch. And for a while at least, Xfm was the coolest place in town to work. It had offices on London's Charlotte Street right in the heart of the new 'media village' springing up just west of Tottenham Court Road. And the offices were a revolving door for new talent. Christian O'Connell, Ricky Gervais, Stephen Merchant, Jimmy Carr, Justin Lee Collins, Lauren Laverne and Zoe Ball all had shows on the station in that gilded era. As, of course, did Russell Brand, the man whose career would ultimately cast a worrying shadow over Dermot's.

Life at Xfm went well for around a year. But then a few changes to the playlists began to grate. The station bosses wanted to play more and more music and leave less and less time for their DJs to talk. But however much he loves music, Dermot loves talking more. He didn't like the feeling that his personality was being eased off the air. So after one more year he and Xfm parted company. To this day everyone concerned is vague about exactly why the break happened – and what the terms of the departure were. But Dermot puts it all down to experience. And as it turned out his timing could hardly have been better.

He had got these two years of extra radio work on to his CV just before the airwaves changed forever. A new gravy train was about to leave the sidings – and Dermot now had the skills and the experience to climb aboard.

Looking back, media experts are still puzzled by the sudden re-emergence of radio as a cultural force. For years the commentators had felt it was an industry in a long-standing and irreversible decline. Everyone's best guess was that video would indeed kill the radio star. And if it didn't do it then some other newer, sexier invention would deal the final blow.

In the first few years of the new millennium all this conventional wisdom was turned on its head. Old jokes about the airwaves being populated solely by those with 'the perfect face for radio' were no longer making sense. Suddenly, it was cool to be on the air. The beautiful people had moved in and radio was sexy – perhaps for the first time in its history. Dermot's old mate Jamie Theakston was one of the first to set the trend at Heart FM, Johnny Vaughan did the same at Capital – and a host of other cool television names soon followed suit. There was Edith Bowman, Sara Cox, Zoe Ball, Richard Bacon, Katy Hill – all going back to the future and getting radio shows on a growing number of FM stations. And while he is the first to admit he's not exactly a looker, Chris Evans was also making radio cool – and proving that television wasn't the be all and end all of the entertainment industry.

Two key things were attracting star names back to radio. The first, and the most obvious, was money. The new stations were flush with cash and desperate to poach the best talent from each other. Radio expert and *Daily Mail* writer Molly Watson pointed to Jamie Theakston's estimated £300,000-a-year wage from Heart as an obvious example of how the industry had changed. 'That's a salary that would have been unthinkable in the industry a decade ago,' she said.

Steve Ackerman, another radio expert and director of production company Somethin' Else, said the second key reason for radio's rebirth was the relaxed nature of the job. 'From the talent's perspective, radio is a much freer medium. It's more intimate and presenters are not someone else's mouthpiece reading from an autocue.' Another benefit is that the presenters can get away with much shorter working days. Chris Tarrant famously said he loved working on Capital because he could roll in at 5.45am and be on the air by 6. 'As a presenter you don't have to spend hours in hair and make-up being beautified and practising for the cameras,' said Ackerman. 'There is still immense pressure to perform, but there is a lot more of the fun and a lot less of the hassle that goes with it. Jonathan Ross's television show is probably a couple of days commitment to rehearsals and research but for his radio programme he needs less time to prepare and he can probably leave the building within an hour of finishing it.'

The final attraction of radio was that it was no longer a backwater or a poor relation to TV. Jonathan Ross averages around 3.5 million listeners for his Radio Two show on a Saturday. That's only around a million less than his *Friday Night With Jonathan Ross* show on BBC One. And experts say radio listeners tend to be more loyal. If you want a long career they are worth courting – as former *Sun* editor Kelvin MacKenzie pointed out when Dermot was considering his next career move. Kelvin had become chairman of Talk Radio and pointed to the relative longevity of radio stars' careers.

'The truth is that TV is a fickle business. It chews you up and spits you out and you can count the number of celebrities who have had 25-year careers on one hand. You might make a six-part series and be great or make two series and be a household name. But sooner or later you'll have bad reviews for something and be out.' he said. Radio, in contrast, lets you settle down, get your feet under the desk and practically earn a good pension. That's another reason why being on the radio is now a goal in itself,' he says. 'Presenters and their agents know that to maximise their exposure and their income they need to spread themselves widely.'

So, in the summer of 2004 Dermot's agent took a series of calls from Radio Two. The station was buckling under its old-fogey reputation. But it was in the middle of a massive re-positioning exercise to attract a whole new demographic of listener. What it wanted was a whole new demographic of presenter. And Dermot's latest television show proved he was the right man, in the right place, doing exactly the right thing. The show was *Re:covered* and it was to take him back to his television roots in Hammersmith, west London, where Dermot had begun his career as a runner. *Re:covered* was recorded at the famous Riverside Studios by the Thames – and Dermot loved it from the start. 'There are a heck of a lot more places to get a sandwich and a coffee now,' he joked with colleagues when he was asked how it felt to be back in west London. The idea for *Re:covered* was hinted at in the show title. Dermot and his team would get today's big acts to perform one of their own tracks and then a cover version of their choice.

The first series went out on Sunday nights on BBC Three – the new name for the old BBC Choice – and it certainly began with a bang. Dermot and his team had sold their idea well. Their promises and cajoling had won the Pet Shop Boys, Natalie Imbruglia and the Stereophonics on the first show. All the acts performed live and as the weeks went by the play list remained stellar – and refreshingly eclectic. The one thing

Dermot is proud to say he will never be is a snob. So he was happy to have acts like Garbage, Blue, Mis-Teeq, Gabrielle and Jamiroquai on the same bill. Mixing it all up made for great music and good TV. Dermot loved it.

The second series, which went out on a more credible Friday night slot, had the likes of Robert Plant, Jamelia, Dirty Vegas, Craig David, Atomic Kitten, Macy Gray, Mel C and Athlete. Ratings weren't huge – they never would be on a minority channel like BBC Three. But Dermot totally loved the whole production process – and he loved spending time with the bands. He was increasingly seeing music people as his kind of people. The sporty little boy who had always felt a little like an outsider was thrilled to be hanging out with these genuinely cool people.

And his work was getting noticed. The show was nominated for a Golden Rose at what was then the Montreux television festival – a nomination that would give vital credibility to Dermot's bid to spread his wings and become a 'broadcaster' rather than a presenter in the years ahead. Back in 2004 that nomination certainly impressed the bosses at Radio Two. They wanted Dermot's credibility. They wanted his contacts book. And most of all they wanted his fans.

When the contact negotiations were over and Dermot was about to be unveiled as a new Radio Two presenter he realised he was in very good company. Alongside the grand old men of the station like Terry Wogan, there were the likes of Jonathan Ross, Steve Wright, Mark Lamarr, Stuart Maconie and Mariella Frostrup.

Dermot's arrival was certainly high profile. He and his

new colleagues filmed a whole series of television adverts for the station. The most famous saw a bike-riding – and helmet-wearing – Dermot zip around the London streets to the studio where he sat on the back of a sofa surrounded by Terry, Mariella, Jonathan and the others. He was clearly the brightest, youngest new face in the line-up, the one the bosses hoped would really attract the new generation in their sights.

But would the gamble pay off?

In September 2004, with the promotion done, it was down to business. *Dermot's Saturday Club* was given the 2pm slot and was broadcast live from the BBC's Portland Place studios. But how to start? Dermot had wanted to play Bruce Springsteen's 'Thunder Road' as his first single. Then someone told him they thought that Jeremy Vine had recently opened his new show with that one. So Dermot went back to his music collection and decided to toss a coin between a Johnny Cash and a Glen Campbell song instead. Also in his early play lists were songs from Bruce Springsteen and another of Dermot's teenage heroes, Paul Weller. Choices like these didn't always do much for Dermot's 'cool young man' image, even though Cash was back in fashion after the Oscar-winning film *Walk the Line*, and Weller had never really lost his edge. But Dermot did soon pick up the pace. Yes, he played plenty of classics from yesteryear, but the big selling point of his new show wasn't the records he choose. It would be the live bands he invited into the studio.

Over the years he has called up most of the bands and performers who appeared on *Re:covered*. And he has put the word out to any number of other established acts. More important still are the new acts he and his team discover. He has developed an increasing passion for edgy outfits that he thinks can break into the musical mainstream. Very often he has been right. The full list of performers to date would run into several pages. And despite his predictions and hopes some have simply faded from view and have never been heard of since. But the big names endure. He's had everyone from Oasis, Moby and Lily Allen through to Massive Attack, Kate Nash and Orson.

But for all this, it has to be said that Dermot's early months on Radio Two weren't an unqualified success. Radio experts said that for some time there was something missing when Dermot was on the air. At the start his show didn't have the 'must listen' or 'go to' quality of his old hero, Jonathan Ross, on a Saturday morning. Nor did it have the manic sense of artfully engineered car-crash radio of his new nemesis, Russell Brand, who at the time was in the Saturday night slot.

Most of Dermot's weekend colleagues had solid identities on their shows – or their programmes had specific fan bases which could be relied upon to tune in and pay attention. Radio fans say veteran broadcaster Paul Gambaccini's fascination with American acts will always have a home. Then it is clear that certain people will always listen to Elaine Paige's show tunes show on a Sunday lunchtime. Whenever these presenters are ill or on holiday regular listeners feel short-changed. But with the best will in the world it was hard to feel that the world would stop turning if Dermot wasn't there for the early days of his afternoon programme.

It soon became clear that he needed to stamp more of an identity on the show. And he decided to do so in his now tried-and-tested fashion. He would have a laugh – at his own expense.

The first step in the new strategy was to talk more – because in general the more Dermot talked the more he laughed. He interacted more with his producers and he took more time to chat to the live acts before and after their sets. So would this do the trick? Dermot thought it had. In one of his most famous extended chats he spoofed it up by telling listeners he was massaging the members of The Magic Numbers to ensure they were calm enough to do their set on his show. And this wasn't just a radio gag. Dermot had it all filmed for the podcast so that listeners could go online and see him give the backrubs. Unfortunately for Dermot it wasn't that well received. Plenty of bad comments were posted on sites like YouTube when the short snippet was put there for all to see. 'I hate him and wish him dead,' said one viewer. 'A complete ****ing squirming, talentless imbecile. How did this clown ever get on TV?' asked another.

Fortunately, all those years after reading his first online critics on the 'more annoying than Mick Hucknall' website, Dermot was finally able to deal with and dismiss this sort of chatter. And there was never really any point in the public trying to mock him. Because he was always one step ahead and ready to do it himself. 'You're voting for your favourite tracks now – in your tens,' he joked one particularly quiet afternoon when listeners didn't seem quite as excited about his contest as he had hoped. Away from the studio Dermot also raised a few smiles with a 'blink and you'll miss him' moment in the video for McFly's 'It's All About You' (he's playing the trombone).

Jokes apart, Dermot knew that hard work and grim determination could see him through this latest career challenge. He believed in his material and in the structure of his show. He knew that his love of good new music was genuine. So he was prepared to tough it out until everyone else got the message. His rationale was simple – and had been with him all his life. Once more, it was that respect has to be earned. Being an overnight success on Radio Two would have been wonderful. But being a success after a long hard slog was actually a lot more satisfying. And in time he did indeed win the battle.

Look back over all his years on Radio Two and his roster of live acts prove he has a surprisingly good ear for new talent. So good, in fact, that his bosses decided to extend the Dermot O'Leary studio sessions brand and package the best sets in a series of double albums. The first of the releases, *The Saturday Sessions*, actually earned Dermot some of the best reviews of his career. Buyers applauded the choice of artists, which ran from Amy Winehouse, Supergrass and Mika to Gomez, Nerina Pallot and Rufus Wainwright. 'Who knew Dermot was so diverse? He's produced a brilliant live album here,' wrote one fan on an online shopping site. 'This album is totally perfect. A rare mix of music and a treasure trove of live performances. This is what we have all been missing in a world of over-hyped, over-produced performers who couldn't sing live if you paid them a million dollars,' wrote another.

It all helped place Dermot more firmly on the music map.

He took to surprising his producers by turning up to work in a shirt and tie (and occasionally in a suit). It's funny, really, that he sometimes liked to dress far more formally for radio than he had ever done for television. But maybe that was because he loved it so much. 'It's one of the favourite things that I do,' he says of Radio 2. 'My producer Ben and I get to play all the music we love. What more could you want?'

Sure, his show still lies in the shadow of its wilder neighbours – not least when Jonathan Ross and Russell Brand hit the headlines after broadcasting the now infamous messages they left on actor Andrew Sachs' answering machine in 2008.

But Dermot can now claim a large and loyal listenership. So when the Saturday schedules were moved around, there was never any question that Dermot's show would be dropped. It was simply moved to a later slot. Best of all, Radio 2's research proved that listeners had started to notice when Dermot took a holiday. He had finally made the show his own.

CHAPTER 14

GOODBYE BIG BROTHER?

It was in the late spring of 2006 that Dermot and Dee grabbed a quick break in the Florida sunshine. They flew business class and checked into a gloriously decadent hotel in Miami's most chic, art deco neighbourhood. Then they hit the beach.

Dee had just finished work on one of her biggest shows to date – as an assistant producer on Channel 4's celebrity-based magic and stunt show *Dirty Tricks*. She was weighing up a vague offer for a future show, *Shipwrecked*, which would involve many weeks away from home out in the Cook Islands. And she was considering several other offers from production companies such as Endemol.

Dermot, meanwhile, had an even bigger decision to make. He was trying to work out if he was approaching the end of the *Big Brother* road. Should he do one more series, then quit while he was still at the top of his game, just as he had done on *T4*? And if he did so, would he ever get to work on such a big show again?

He knew Dee's advice would be sound as he mulled over the decision. But he didn't want his career crisis to cast a cloud over their trip. And Dee didn't want to spend too much of her short break worrying about work either. So after one final discussion on the beach they decided to focus on something else: having fun. Fortunately both of them are good at making the most of the here and now. Both are even better at letting their hair down when career commitments allow. So when they went snorkelling one day and met two American tourists called Terry and Joe the scene was set for a whole lot of laughs.

'They were enormous and the funniest men alive,' remembers Dermot. 'They took us out for dinner. Then we said, "Come back to our hotel for a drink". And we ran up an enormous bar bill.' The next day, Dermot admits, it was all a bit of a blur, though he doesn't think he ever got too loud or lairy as the booze flowed. 'I'm a very happy drunk. I just get all cuddly,' he laughs. What he and Dee had enjoyed the most about the trip was their total anonymity. To Terry and Joe they were just another British couple with funny accents and an open mini bar. They weren't media figures or tabloid targets. It had been a refreshing change. Though Dermot, in particular, flew back to Britain as unsure about his future as he had been the day he left. He was committed to at least one more *Big Brother* and *Celebrity Big Brother* series. And he was about to totally revamp his programme. But after that? The jury remained out.

Heat reporter Lucie Cave, who met Dermot at a photoshoot within hours of his plane landing back at Heathrow, says there were few signs that he was uncertain about his future.

She remembers him as looking a little jet-lagged but being as charming as ever. He fussed around a group of photography students who were on work experience seeing how a professional shoot is managed. He chatted happily to the camera crew and laughed away with the make-up lady. And then he gave Lucie his full attention.

The purpose of the interview and the pictures was to promote the next *Big Brother* show. But everyone connected to the shoot – and everyone reading Dermot's words in this and other interviews that spring – could sense a slight change of tone. Was Dermot's passion for the show starting to wane?

'I still love *Big Brother* but it has become more difficult to defend it as the years have gone on. I can't really say to journalists, "These people get psychologically vetted. They don't let people who are unstable into the house", because they can now turn around and say, "Michael Barrymore" and I pretty much lose the argument,' he said. And even when he was asked to elaborate, and to accept the way the media works, his words weren't as convincing as they had been in the past. 'Yes, *Big Brother* pays for edgy shows like *Shameless*. That has to be worth something,' he said weakly. 'Apart from that it is probably the best case study in human behaviour you can imagine. The conspiracy theorists who always think it's set up? I'd love to just bring them down to the studio and say, Do you think we're that organised? *Big Brother* is still a valid social experiment. You just have to look harder for it,' he concluded.

So why the change of heart?

In truth there was more to it than the increasing media-awareness and naked ambition of each year's housemates. It wasn't just the inmates of the house who had changed. Something had changed in Dermot's world as well.

In television, nothing lasts forever. No one stays hot for long. There is always someone else just behind snapping at your heels and riding a whole new zeitgeist. For Dermot, in 2006, that person was Russell Brand. Until Russell came along Dermot had mopped up every bit of *Big Brother* interest after Davina had enjoyed her say. His show was the one and only choice for *Big Brother* obsessives who wanted more than the evictions and the standard fix of housemate-related gossip.

But when Russell hit the scene Dermot found someone else's tanks on his lawn.

Russell was a sensation as far back as 2004 when he introduced E4 viewers to *Big Brother's Big Mouth*. It was the wildest, most outspoken and most off-the-wall show in the *Big Brother* family. It got even wilder when it was moved to a post-watershed slot the following year. And Russell himself was mesmerising. His comments were pure 'water cooler' television, endlessly repeated the next day in schools and workplaces. From very small beginnings he became a huge word of mouth hit. Could Dermot really compete with that?

'You always have to deal with new stuff coming along and new people suddenly getting big and getting all the attention. I don't begrudge them at all,' he said. But was this really true? The secret steel that has always kept Dermot standing would not allow him to see *BBLB* just roll over and die. 'I want it to be "the" Friday night show,' he told his production team as they got ready for the 2006 season. 'We have to keep it fresh,' he said. He wanted the highest ratings and the best reviews. He wanted to face off his new challenger.

One idea to keep Dermot ahead of the curve was the 2006 launch of the live psychological programme, *Big Brother's Brain*. This would let him take a more considered look at what was going on in the house by questioning the housemates actions and motivations. It would all be done with the lightest of touches. But it would be a touch more grown-up than the rants on *Big Brother's Big Mouth*. So would *Brain* be a new lease of life for Dermot? Would it confirm his place at the top of the reality tree?

Not quite. Just before the show's first broadcast, in May 2006, Dermot's supporters were horrified when they saw the results of a set of Channel 4 photo-shoots designed to promote that summer's show. In the main image that was reprinted everywhere Dermot was marooned, standing behind Davina with his arms folded. But Davina's position – up front and central – wasn't the real problem. Nor was it that she had her back to him. What Dermot's fans didn't like was the fact that Russell was there as the third person in the reality relationship. 'It was like Charles, Diana and Camilla, all over again,' remembers one fan.

And Russell was impossible to ignore. Davina was smiling broadly as she held on to the lapels of his jacket. The overall dynamic was clear. He was the focus of the whole shoot. He was the one who drew everyone's eyes. The wild-haired newcomer was now the star of the show. If a picture is worth a thousand words then these repeated one key message: that Russell was now the main man. Dermot had been pushed into the sidelines. And for all his relaxed charm, that wasn't a place he liked to be.

It meant that when Grace, Nikki, Pete, Aisleyne, Shahbaz and co. all entered the *Big Brother* house that summer, Dermot went to work on rebuilding his reputation. *BBLB* was as manic and endearing as ever. Dermot's rapport with his guests was just as strong. And he was about to be given a very big vote of confidence from the Channel 4 top brass.

In 2006 Davina was pregnant with her third child. And once more the birth was due just after the end of the series. Everyone knew the producers had to have a replacement in place in case she went into labour early. But who would they choose? In 2001 and 2003 Dermot had been the obvious choice. But in 2006 a rumour swept the industry saying that this time it would be Russell. If the stories could be believed this would be a very public demotion – and a total humiliation – for Dermot.

That rumour proved to be false. It was indeed Dermot who was put on standby to take over the main Channel 4 show – with its live evictions and eviction interviews – should Davina dip out. In the end baby Chester didn't arrive until Pete was safely unveiled as the latest *Big Brother* winner. Later that year Dermot hammed it up – and dragged it up – by wearing a replica of Princess Nikki's red dress and recreating her tear-stained and extraordinarily emotional exit from the *Big Brother* house for *Heat* magazine's end-of-year issue. The pictures were sensational. But still Russell managed to upstage him. Turn the page from Dermot in a dress and there was Mr Brand holding a sword and cutlass and looking every inch like Johnny Depp in *Pirates of the Caribbean*.

As they looked at the pictures, Dermot's keenest fans may have worried if he could ever reverse this tide and reclaim his former glory. Maybe that would be even harder to do if the whole *Big Brother* bubble was truly about to burst. Stunts that might have made every fan smile a few years ago were starting to grate today. Not everything looked as fun as it should.

'What's the worst moment of your professional life to date?' Dermot was asked. He looked back to *Big Brother 5* (incidentally, Russell Brand's first year on the show) and said it was interviewing Marco in the paddling pool. For a start, Dermot thought he himself looked just a little pale and a tiny bit fat when he saw the playbacks. 'Because of health and safety the paddling pool couldn't be filled up in case it broke. We didn't have any bath foam so I ended up in a paddling pool in a couple of inches of water, with washing up liquid in it, all going right up my backside. It was horrible,' he said. Surely, a few years earlier, washing up liquid or not, that paddling pool scene with someone as outrageous as Marco would have been fun? Now it was on Dermot's list as a career low. Something imperceptible must have changed. But what could be done about it?

The good news was that the more he thought about it the less he wanted Russell Brand's life in the first place. He remembers one conversation with the fellow star, who had been talking about being plagued by the paparazzi – and loving it. Dermot simply couldn't see the attraction. 'I just thought: "Go home. Shut the door. Or go and watch West Ham." I wouldn't want to live his kind of life at all.' But Russell was always ready to up the ante. 'May I say, explicitly and without any duplicity: I like being famous. I like it. I did it on purpose. I did it quite, quite deliberately. I went into it with my eyes open and I won't rest until there is not a single territory on this planet where I cannot go to a supermarket. Obscurity doesn't suit me.'

In some ways it seemed to suit Dermot, however. Though he wasn't ready to sink into it just yet.

The other good news after the worrisome summer on *Big Brother 7* was that Dermot was certainly not short of employment opportunities. He happily presented a few more of the 'best-of' shows for *Big Brother* as he did most years. Then there was something else. Producers had come up with the idea of a *Big Brother All Stars* series for the following year with a few dozen of the best – and worst – housemates from all seven previous series. A twist was that Dermot, Davina, and Russell Brand, would all enter the house at different stages of the show. The staff trying to book the housemates knew full well that Dermot was on record saying he would never do reality television. Going further, he had once said he would 'hack off my own arm' before going on *Celebrity Big Brother*. But that was then. In the new climate might he not face up to the inevitable need to keep winning new fans? Might he not accept that any work was better than none?

'He is beginning to come around to the idea since he already knows all of the potential contestants and wouldn't be forced to live with people he didn't get on with. We know it's a long shot but it would make an amazing show,' one insider told the press. What was left unsaid was the thought that Dermot might change his mind because he knew he needed to adapt to the new landscape of reality television. He needed to put a firework up his own career to keep him up in the sky. But as it turned out Dermot stuck to his guns. He said 'no' to *Big Brother All Stars* – and soon the producers lost interest as well.

With this project stone dead Dermot's key aim was to move on from reality television altogether. And fortunately his hard-fought freelance status allowed him to pick and choose his projects and flit from one channel to another at will.

Being given work by the BBC and ITV as well as Channel 4 was a huge boost to his confidence. Surely somewhere, he asked himself, I will get the chance to do something completely different and originate a big show of my own? For while he was widely seen as the *T4* and *BBLB* presenter, he was very aware that he had taken over the former from Ben Shephard and had originally presented the latter as part of a duo with Natalie Casey. What he wanted – still wanted – was what Terry Wogan and Jonathan Ross had: personal triumphs that they had created and launched single-handedly.

Immediately after *Big Brother 7*, Dermot had been building up hopes of doing just this at the BBC. He had been offered one of the biggest platforms on the Beeb – a new Saturday night *National Lottery* game show. Winning that gig was the gold standard of prime-time television. Anthea Turner, Bob Monkhouse, Eamonn Holmes and Dale Winton had all been given it. Now Dermot O'Leary's name went on the roster. So that was a clear riposte to everyone who'd said Dermot's star was on the wane, right? It should have been. Especially as the show looked like being a whole lot of fun.

It was called *National Lottery: 1 vs 100* – and Dermot was to be its first-ever host. He filmed eight shows in October 2006 and was asked back to film a second short series the following spring. The callback seemed the biggest vote of confidence of all. But in truth *1 vs 100* wasn't an entirely unqualified success. Yes, it got more than seven million viewers – a career high for Dermot. But most of them were only really watching to check their lucky numbers. Many may well have watched if the BBC had put a monkey in the quizmaster's chair.

Worse was the fact that critics said Dermot seemed ill at ease in the straightjacket of the quiz show format and needed more flexibility for his true personality to come out. A media row over a poppy-less Dermot on Remembrance Weekend also created unnecessary controversy. And television conspiracy theorists also pointed out that while Dermot was now on the BBC he wasn't entirely out of his professional comfort zone. They had spotted the fact that *1 vs 100* was made by good old Endemol, the *Big Brother* creator that had given Dermot all his best gigs to date. Once more questions were asked about whether Dermot could ever really hack it out of the reality television shadow. And once more he was set to face a lot more of the criticism that had always dogged his career. It seemed that he had made himself a target all over again by going on Saturday night television. And a lot of people were lining up to take shots at him.

One of the first critics got personal. He said Dermot's short hair made his head 'resemble a potato' And it wasn't just Dermot who was under fire. So too were his female fans. 'Working with the depressingly obvious formula that "bloke on TV plus trips to the gym equals sex symbol" O'Leary has pumped his pecs with enthusiasm. The resultant buffness has had women, who would normally know better, swooning to his stumpy, spuddy charms,' wrote Andrew Williams in London freesheet *Metro*. And to prove he wasn't being shallow by only attacking the way Dermot looked, Williams then moved on to his body of work. 'Only Davina McCall has got dodgier, more instantly forgettable TV fodder on her show reel. If you can recall seeing this bunch of veg-out no-brainers: *No Balls Allowed*, *The Bigger Breakfast*, *The Dog's Balearics*, *Big Brother's Little Brother*, *SAS: Are You Tough Enough?* or *Re:covered*, you're either a square-eyed shut-in or Dermot's mum.'

Sticks and stones, sticks and stones. That was how Dermot took this latest piece of criticism. And for once it was a lot easier to face down the insults. Because he had just agreed to film one very exciting new show and had received one very important phone call. The new show was ITV's *Extinct* – in which a group of celebrities championed endangered species and explained why special efforts had to be made to save them. Dermot's focus was on the leatherback turtle and he got to fly out to Costa Rica to see the animals in their natural habitat. Producers on the series say that tight shooting schedules meant the programmes were a lot harder to make than they appeared – they were at pains to scotch rumours that the series was simply a giant jolly, offering rich celebrities the chance to boost their fame while having yet another free holiday. Dermot stayed silent on all this. Maybe it was just because he had done so much live and recorded television by now. Maybe it was because he was genuinely interested in conservation and had already read a great deal about his subject. But in some ways *Extinct* did seem a little like a lovely sunny holiday.

And when he got back he had that vital phone call to focus upon. It seemed that after nearly two years of uncertainty he finally looked set to win the big new job of his dreams. If all went well in the next few months then absolutely everything in Dermot's life was going to change forever.

CHAPTER 15

THE X FACTOR

It was mid-April in 2007 when a smart but low-key Dermot O'Leary climbed out of his cab at Heathrow Airport and headed to the International Departures hall. He was checking in for a scheduled flight out to Los Angeles and was hoping that no one on board would recognise him. He was lucky. Only a few people spotted him as he walked across the airport concourse and headed through security and into the private executive lounge. No one bothered him, asked for an autograph or – crucially – asked where he was flying to.

Once inside the airport lounge he certainly didn't look like any of the other harassed-looking business men with laptop bags and crumpled suits. Nor did he look like the well-heeled tourists upgrading for a more luxury start to their holiday. So what, exactly, was the purpose of his trip? At US immigration everyone has to answer the 'business or pleasure' question. And Dermot's answer didn't come easily – because in truth it was a bit of both.

When he got through immigration and walked through the

arrivals hall at LAX there was a car waiting to take him to his hotel. The next day he was driven to CBS Television City in Fairfax, Los Angeles to watch Ryan Seacrest host the latest edition of *American Idol*. The sun was shining and the streets were lined with palm trees. But apart from that it was Shepherd's Bush Green and Terry Wogan all over again. Dermot was ready to learn from an expert. Simon Cowell had asked him to see just how well Ryan controlled his show. He wanted Dermot to do exactly the same back in Britain with *The X Factor*.

The former pop reporter Kate Thornton had shocked TV insiders by winning the plumb *X Factor* job back in 2004. It was a tough gig, stepping into the joint shadow of Ant and Dec who had effectively done the same job on *Pop Idol*. And poor Kate had walked into an immediate chorus of disapproval. She didn't have a huge amount of television experience, especially on big budget, live programmes. At best she was attacked for her fashion sense – or apparent lack of it. In 2005 Jonathan Ross won one of the biggest laughs of the night at the Comedy awards by poking fun at her 'stylist'. More seriously, other critics simply felt she was too wooden for mainstream television and too weak to control the wild egos of her three warring judges. The ITV executives had been happy for her to have the whole of the first series to win over her critics. They gave her the second series to put down further roots on the show. But after seeing Leona Lewis win the third show in 2006 it was revealed that she wouldn't come back the following year.

The big question was who could replace her. The show was

a massive hit, with up to 12 million viewers and a solid foundation on the Saturday night schedules. But its producers knew they couldn't afford to make a second mistake. If Kate were to go, then her replacement had to be right.

Simon, the power behind every aspect of the show, said that the replacement had to be a man. He felt the dynamic worked better that way. And that's why he wanted Dermot to see Ryan Seacrest in the flesh in LA. Ryan might not always win the best reviews – in fact he has come in for as much criticism stateside as Kate did in the UK. But Simon never lost faith in him. And he thought he could see the same magic in Dermot. As a quick aside, Dermot does laugh about the fact that the whole point of his trip to LA was to be totally discreet. At this point no one knew exactly who might step into Kate's shoes and that was how Simon wanted things to stay. But Dermot made one mistake – he got caught by the *American Idol* cameras. If you look very carefully at the show in question you can see him in the back of one audience shot, clapping along to a Jon Bon Jovi track – something his mates still laugh about to this day.

Having been rumbled on camera, the need for secrecy was reduced. So Dermot was allowed out of the shadows. That night he went to dinner at Robert de Niro's Italian restaurant Ago on Melrose Avenue. He was joining Simon and two other very high-profile people: Jerry Springer and *Daily Mirror* editor turned *Britain's Got Talent* judge Piers Morgan. Jerry, of course, knows everything there is about being a success on TV. And Piers was catching up fast. As well as his UK work he was making a big name for himself in

America where he had won another judging role on *America's Got Talent*. Dermot must surely have been in his element. He was having a business dinner with television's elite and his talent was in demand. From his humble beginnings in Essex he was now in LA with movers and shakers. The luck of the Irish certainly seemed to be with him as Simon explained, at another meeting which followed, why he wanted the talented presenter. 'He said something very interesting,' Dermot would later reveal. 'He said, "We want you to do this job because you like people." I'd never really thought of it like that before. But I can talk the hind legs off a donkey.'

Just as important was what Simon always referred to as 'the likeability factor'. He knew that people liked the smiling, Tiggerish Irishman. They responded to his enthusiasm, his humour, even his on-air mistakes. They felt that he was on their side – that he too was excited about the shows he presented and the people he met. That was the magic Simon wanted to scatter across the *X Factor* studio. 'Dermot is warm, clever and funny. He is the natural choice for the show, simple as that,' he said when he was asked why he had considered Dermot in the first place. But even as he spoke, Dermot was still to agree to the job. Informal talks continued for a while after Dermot's return from LA.

One report said they sealed the deal during a late night drive through London in Simon's Rolls Royce. If true, it must have been a bizarre and surreal drive. And it fired the starting pistol on a huge new opportunity for Dermot. Sure, he had lived a great life and earned a lot of money to date. But this was the big league. It was also the next big challenge he had been looking for. So what could he say? Nothing. Apart from, 'Yes. I'm in. When do we start?'

It's not often that Louis Walsh agrees with Simon Cowell. But he did agree that Dermot was the right man to follow in Kate's footsteps. 'He has the looks, the humour and is a very warm and genuine person. He is the best male presenter in the country today. Plus, he's Irish,' he said with a smile. And all the other top brass in television seemed to agree. 'He was our Number One choice,' confirmed ITV controller of entertainment Duncan Gray. And it seems the channel had been prepared to pay top dollar to ensure it got its way. Insiders pointed to a pay packet put at upwards of £1 million for a two-series deal with an option to stay with the show much longer if all sides agreed. Less than ten years ago Dermot had been sleeping on pals' floors to save money while he tried to get any kind of step onto the broadcasting ladder. Now he was in the entertainment elite. But he certainly hadn't forgotten his roots, or his manners. Ever the gentleman, the day before he officially accepted the job Dermot rang Kate Thornton so she would be the first to know. 'She was very gracious and a lady,' he remembers of their conversation.

Unfortunately for Dermot not everyone took the news so well. When his appointment was confirmed to the press online gossip sites questioned Dermot's ability to really connect with a prime-time audience – especially after his relatively wooden performances on *1 vs 100*. Those who had felt Kate Thornton lacked the necessary charisma for the show were not convinced that Dermot could automatically supply it. The show was all about having the 'X Factor'. But did the new host really provide it?

'He's too wild,' was how one set of online discussions began. 'He won't be able to work in a studio show like that.' 'He's too wooden,' came a much later thread, proving that people's views of Dermot were mixed, to say the least.

It was clear that the jury was out, and that for many Saturday night ITV viewers Dermot himself was something of an unknown quantity. The older mums, dads and grandparents weren't the types to have seen *Big Brother's Little Brother*, let alone *T4* all those years ago. So everyone was preparing to step into the dark in the summer of 2007. And as what initially began as a mild rumbling of dissent looked set to grow into a real storm Dermot became aware of just how large a job he had taken on. *The X Factor* and prime-time Saturday night ITV mattered to people. Viewers felt they had a stake in the show, not least because they paid into it through the money from phone and text votes. So they were a lot more demanding of their hosts.

As he dealt with this pressure Dermot faced something else – something that mattered to him even more. He began to attract some criticism from his peers in the entertainment industry. The barbs thrown his way weren't all directed at his ability, but at his acceptance of such a high-profile, mainstream job. Unnamed sources attacked him for selling out, saying his new job was all about the money and left his artistic credibility in shambles. For once Dermot fought back – publicly. 'Anyone who would turn this down is lying,' he said, at the same time involved in a minor spat with Vernon Kay, who had apparently said he'd done just that.

Meanwhile, other arguments appeared to have been triggered by Dermot's promotion. His old pal Ben Shephard had hoped that when Kate left he could make the leap from *The Xtra Factor* on ITV2 to the main stage. Seeing his former *T4* colleague pip him to the post was something of a shock, and Ben soon left the programme as well, to be replaced by Fearne Cotton. It was a summer of surprises, jealousies and musical chairs. And throughout it all Dermot didn't stop once to consider if he did, indeed, have the fabled 'X Factor'. He would leave that for other people to decide. What he knew he did have was the luck of the Irish. 'I'm just one of those annoying, fortunate people who have been in the right place at the right time. Getting *The X Factor* is like being a Premiership footballer and it's the closest I'll ever come to being a big money signing. I'm going from a middleweight to a heavyweight and at the moment I am just really happy. I hope that doesn't make me sound smug because I'm not. I really do appreciate what I have. But things are going great for me. And I'm not about to shroud it in mystery. I'm hugely flattered to have this job. Work is great and I'm delighted about everything, and that's it.'

The media took about two weeks to settle down after Dermot's new role was announced. As usual, this intensely private man was deluged with interview requests, almost all of which were politely refused. When the series finally began, in the autumn of 2007, he knew he would have a contractual obligation to do some essential publicity for the show. But until then he wanted to keep as low profile as possible. Not least because life was about to get very, very busy.

The national auditions for *The X Factor* took place during the summer of 2007. Which, of course, was *Big Brother* season. A big part of Dermot wished he had followed his gut instincts at the end of the year before and quit the show when he was ahead. But then he decided that he should stop complaining and get on with the job. Sure, it was going to be a logistical nightmare to fulfil all his filming commitments that summer. But he was at least earning a huge wage for the twin tasks. So in a world where ordinary people may work two jobs just to survive he had the good grace to keep quiet. And, on a lighter note, he was energised by the thought that that year's *Big Brother* house could be really worth watching – because apart from former boy-band star Ziggy, the first set of housemates were all going to be female.

As it turned out the experiment wasn't a success. The girls certainly had their moments – and 2007 gave us plenty of tabloid fodder. But somehow the series didn't set the world alight. Dermot and his *BBLB* team had a few worrying times in their Elstree Studios – he still filmed on the famous George Lucas Stage there – trying to keep the show fresh and fun.

And, immediately after most broadcasts, Dermot was then rushed across the country to join his other colleagues on *The X Factor*. He says he only had three days off in the summer of 2007 – and pretty soon the strain was beginning to show. 'I felt that I was about to die,' he said of the sheer exhaustion he felt many days that summer. But as ever this was no diva-like hissy fit, nor a plea for public sympathy. Dermot might have given up a lot of his personal privacy but he would never lose his sense of perspective. 'Now obviously I'm not doing a job where I have to go down the mines or anything. So I don't want to sound too dramatic. But I really did feel I couldn't do both shows justice or be in two places at once,' was how he put it. Not that this stopped his producers from trying. Several times in those manic months the only way the various teams could get him where he needed to be was to hire a helicopter for a day. Sometimes, when this wasn't practical, he was put on the back of a motorbike taxi service so that he could get from one studio to another in time for his next set of production meetings, auditions and film dates

As a footnote, it is worth saying that some television insiders actually felt Dermot was underselling himself by saying how tough it had been filming two high-profile shows at the same time. Throw in *The Xtra Factor* and he was, in fact, filming three, they said. Add in Radio Two and the total becomes four. And pitch in the treadmill of meetings, promotions, photo shoots, interviews, meet-and-greets with competition winners, charity staff and station executives and the pace became relentless.

And while Dermot was comfortable in his *BBLB* world, he had the added edge of dealing with a whole new set of personalities on the vast and intimidating planet of *The X Factor*. Yes, he had won over Simon and Louis. But what about the others? The *X Factor* crew say Dermot visibly blushed when he met Sharon Osbourne for the first time. He has said he's always had a mini crush on that most feisty of ladies and she intended to make the most of his embarrassment.

Auditions for that year's show lasted three months and took place in seven locations around the country. More than 150,000 people would try out for the show that summer – a record number. Many were inspired by last year's big winner, Leona Lewis, who was tipped to become a huge, international star. As a viewer, Dermot had shared everyone's admiration for Leona in 2006. He had loved seeing her talent and confidence develop over the course of that second series. The hope that he might be on the spot when another global superstar emerged was another major reason why he had taken on the top job. 'I would just love to be there when a new star is discovered,' he said. Friends say he has a genuine admiration for anyone who is truly great at their job, whatever that job may be. Spotting new talent would be the biggest rush of all, he said. But would he actually recognise it if he saw it?

Dermot told pals that he remains as baffled as the rest of us over who gets put through to the next rounds and into boot camp. He says he can hardly ever tell who the judges will like or dislike – and when he is convinced that a certain person will be accepted or rejected he is nearly always wrong. Cleverly, Dermot hasn't ever told friends (let alone the public) much about the controversial side of the the *X Factor* audition process – the fact that it would be logistically impossible for more than a tiny minority of hopefuls to be seen on camera by the four key judges. Some nine in ten of the hopefuls are first seen by production staff, who sift through looking for the weird, the wonderful and everyone in between. Most of the hopefuls don't know if Dermot and the judges are in the building at any given time and are very unlikely to meet them even if they are.

The auditions process was one part of previous shows that

Kate had made her own. Surprisingly tactile and empathetic she was always there outside the auditions rooms to celebrate or commiserate with the contestants. Her hugs, kisses, shrieks and tears became her signature actions. But for all his easy, matey style and chatty nature Dermot was never going to be quite as up-close-and-personal with the singers – at least not outside the audition room door.

In his first year on the show Dermot decided he would spend more time with the contestants before they faced the judges. 'I like the ones I can have a bit of banter with,' he said, and he sat down with far more of them in the corridors and holding rooms to hear about their life stories, their dreams and their motivations. 'Most people are really likeable. When I get someone who is a bit brattish I try to inject a bit of realism. When you get people who think they are a lot better than they are you have to gauge your response very carefully,' he says, a diplomat to the end.

His hope was that these pre-audition chats would make a larger part of the final shows, though in the end there simply wasn't the time to show more than a tiny handful of them in the middle of all the car crash sessions in front of the judges. So Dermot was pushed back to the studio doors so he could congratulate and commiserate just as Kate had always done. He didn't necessarily like all the histrionics of the post-audition moments. But he knew that the viewers did. And for Dermot that's always come first.

'The interviews after people have been rejected are always emotionally exhausting,' he revealed. But had he really been there for enough of them? One newspaper report gave Dermot plenty of food for thought. It quoted unnamed 'insiders' saying that Simon Cowell was unhappy with the amount of time that Dermot had dedicated to *Big Brother*. Next year, the story went, Simon expected Dermot to dedicate himself full time to *The X Factor*. Had he read it, Dermot would surely have been stung by the implied criticism in the article. He could also have been mildly offended that someone else was telling him how to organise his life and his career. But he could also have taken something positive from it as well. Long before *The X Factor* had been broadcast, Simon – if the reports were true – had already decided that Dermot would be its host in 2009 and beyond. That was a thought worth holding on to when the exhaustion kicked in during that crazy first summer.

Through it all Dermot did at least try to remain relaxed. In the middle of August, when *Big Brother* was in full swing, he headed to central London for the huge press launch for that year's *The X Factor*. It was held at a glitzy Mayfair hotel and after all the rumours of rows among the judges (and the question of whether Louis would remain part of the show) media interest was intense. Dermot actually arrived early, much to the surprise of the ITV staff and the events organisers who were busy getting the room ready. They remember that their high-profile new star and a couple of his pals happily headed to the bar while they waited for everyone else to turn up. Dermot, it was clear, was not going to be a high-maintenance colleague.

And as the day passed, Dermot could at least relax in the knowledge that *Big Brother 8* would soon be behind him. So on 31 August 2007, when fellow Essex boy Brian Belo walked out of the house as the eighth *Big Brother* winner, Dermot was on an extraordinary high. He was looking forward to interviewing the man he had liked from the start of the series. But after that he was looking forward to having a very good night's sleep. Now that *BBLB* was over he could put all his energy into *The X Factor*. Half the workload, the same amount of energy. What could possibly go wrong?

CHAPTER 16

BOOT CAMPS AND LIVE SHOWS

The auditions bandwagon rolled on after *BBLB* ended and *The X Factor* boot camp began. For the first time, all the judges stayed together as the number of performers was halved, and halved again. They judged the acts in a country park hotel in Oxfordshire and a theatre on London's Shaftesbury Avenue. After that the travelling began again in earnest. It was to film in the judges' homes and Dermot had to zip from Marbella with Simon, to Los Angeles with Sharon, to Ibiza with Dannii and to Dublin with Louis.

And all the time he needed to prepare for the most important moment of all. The live shows that would dominate ITV's autumn schedules. 'This is a big, big beast, the biggest show on television,' he admitted. And he knew too that it was also the most challenging. It was broadcast live. It was ITV's flagship show with more than ten million viewers. Dermot had to own that studio from the outset, the way he had seen Terry Wogan own the room all those years ago at the Shepherd's Bush Theatre.

But Dermot had a lot more to worry about than Terry. There were an awful lot of links to get right. The timing had to be spot on. The judges had to be kept in line and the contestants – understandably terrified of doing live performances – needed to be supported through the ordeal. The list of potential problems for the host was long. There was vast scope for messing up. Not for nothing are Ant and Dec so well respected – and so well paid. 'Only a tiny number of people can really control a juggernaut like *Pop Idol*, *I'm A Celebrity* or *The X Factor*,' says producer Martin Reynolds, who has worked on many of the country's biggest live shows. 'It requires nerves of steel and an intense concentration. You need to be firm but very, very flexible. And you must never let the audience know how hard you're working.' And as if all this wasn't tough enough, Dermot had two extra hurdles to clear. First, he knew that as the new host all eyes would be on him to see if he could truly handle the challenge. Second, in an industry still reeling from the scandal of fraudulent premium rate phone votes, he knew that the regulators as well as the viewers would be watching every move he made.

'You've got to want to prove yourself on a bigger stage and that's why I took it on,' he said of the show that autumn. But when he had signed his contract he hadn't quite realised just how big that stage would be. What had been in his mind was *The X Factor* time slot. Dermot says he has never been personally jealous of rival presenters as people – but he is jealous of the prime time slots they often command. Going to *The X Factor* gave him the Saturday night showcase he had always wanted. The National Lottery show had given him a taste of this status. Now he could eat his fill of it. And he did feel ready. He had one message for the people who thought he couldn't cope with the live shows. It was that no one could beat him when it came to experience. Sure, *BBLB* might not have hit the wider national consciousness or attracted a mainstream, ITV-style audience. But Dermot's shows had been relentless, live and high pressure. One of his professional mottos is: 'Instinct is Everything', and he had always put that to the test on *BBLB*. He would do so again on *The X Factor*.

His natural fitness would surely see him through. He had pretty much stopped drinking when he was racing between the *BBLB* shows and *The X Factor* auditions that summer. When others might have been in a hotel bar he was in the gym or out pounding the streets. Back in London Dermot also took on a new personal trainer and started boxing lessons, having been told that few other sports push you as hard, or keep you in as good a shape. In the autumn, every performer and television presenter becomes paranoid about coughs and colds. The whole industry tries hard to eat and sleep properly and make sure some virus doesn't make their lives even more difficult.

One week to the live shows and Dermot was still thinking long and hard about what kind of host he would be. He had spent hours at home watching tapes of the first three series, and of similar shows from around the world. Yes, instinct was important. But preparation would be everything as well. So he didn't leave anything to chance.

His first big decision was about the exact nature of his role.

Would he side with the judges or with the performers? 'The performers,' he said, without missing a beat. 'If anyone has a go at the contestants I'll stick up for them because I'm their buddy and that's my job,' he said. And how would he cope with Simon, Sharon, Louis and newcomer Dannii? 'If they start causing trouble I'll definitely be answering back,' he claimed, not altogether convincingly. He might have coped alongside the SAS in his BBC series, but standing up to Simon Cowell was probably going to take much sterner stuff. Not everyone was sure that Dermot had what it took.

As they considered the question some felt that Simon had picked Dermot because he knew that the newcomer wouldn't answer back too much. Was Simon's belief that a soft, nervous new host would allow the spotlight to stay firmly focused on him? Would it ensure that Simon could speak for longer than his fellow judges and not get picked up on any inconsistencies in his statements?

What Simon didn't know was that Dermot had already come up with a clever way to keep the show's most famous judge in check. He'd decided he would be able to diffuse Simon's more outrageous comments by subtly taking the mickey out of him. He felt that a raised eye-brow here or a face-pull to the audience there would keep Simon in check and show viewers that Dermot was his own man. He'd pulled a few of those faces in that last week's rehearsals. He just hoped he could keep his nerve and do the same when the heat – and the cameras – were on.

One day before the live shows and Dermot did something very unusual. He faced the paparazzi in Central London.

BOOT CAMPS AND LIVE SHOWS

The media buzz about the new series confirmed that taking on the lead presenter's role would change Dermot's life. But what kind of effect might it have on those closest to him? Could his low profile relationship with Dee be affected? Could their relative anonymity be destroyed? In all their time together they had rarely been photographed as a couple and while many of Dermot's big fans knew he had a girlfriend called Dee very few would have been able to pick her out of a line-up.

Living the quiet life meant they were rarely hassled by journalists. They didn't get reporters sifting through their bins at home or paparazzi snapping them in supermarket car parks. Most editors appreciated that when Dermot said 'no' to an interview request he meant it.

But in 2007 he did have a contractual obligation to meet and greet a little more – and he knew that if *The X Factor* was to stay a hit he had to raise his profile as he raised his game. If the wider public were to like him they needed to know him. It was time to face the cameras. He and Dee dressed up for a rare public appearance the night before the first live show of the series. It meant the papers would be wall-to-wall Dermot on the most important day of his career. The big bash was the *Spiderman 3* premiere in London's Leicester Square and Dermot joked that the outing helped take his mind off the first show the following day. 'I'm nervous, it's that first day at a new school feeling,' he told fans on the edge of the red carpet. Look very closely at the pictures – as many keen fans did – and you can see that Dermot was still looking tired after his long, busy summer. Until now that tiredness had been relatively easy to hide. As long as the make-up teams had done their job and allowed him to sparkle on *BBLB* then it was only the insiders on *The X Factor* who saw the tautness of his skin and shadows under his eyes. Now the whole country was in on the secret. Dermot had to prove he had the stamina to survive. In October 2007 it wasn't just the 12 nervous contestants who were starting to worry about walking on to that wide ITV stage.

A pale but excited Dermot was driven to the Fountain Studios in Wembley, north London just after ten the following day. After a round of greetings and a fair few team hugs he sat down with a coffee and his script. As he wrote notes in the margins, he watched a few of the final rehearsals then talked his latest ideas through with his co-writers. In the first show of the new series there is a lot of explaining to do and not a lot of room for any individuality to show through. But Dermot still wanted as many of his words as possible to come straight from his heart. A few cheeky lines, especially about the judges, would certainly do that.

Just after 3pm Dermot went into make-up. His long-standing make-up artist is a hugely calming influence on him and he loves being made a fuss of in front of the mirrors. It takes his mind off the ticking of the clock. He has a personal stylist, Eve, who checks his clothes are in perfect condition. After seeing Kate face a weekly humiliation over her increasingly odd taste in clothes, Dermot wanted to give the show a slicker, professional look. He and Eve had picked a set of smart, fitted suits. It was the eighties' Jonathan Ross reinvented two decades on.

Unable to take his mind off the clock Dermot did another

backstage tour. Scattered across several shared dressing rooms was the new set of very nervous competitors, the youngest being 15-year-old Emily Nakanda. 'This is more important for them, than it is for me,' was Dermot's attitude. 'It's certainly more nerve-wracking.' What he didn't realise that his very presence was helping them cope. Several have said that it helped enormously to see that they weren't surrounded by steely television professionals and cynical media automatons. They say it was clear that Dermot was as nervous as they were. And that in a strange sort of way this made everything seem a little easier to deal with.

After saying his goodbyes Dermot headed to the galley to talk briefly with a few key crew members. As he did so he looked out on the full rows of seats in the vast studio – the biggest in Britain. It was all a far cry from the intimate room where *BBLB* had been filmed – and it was a world away from the 'broom cupboard' where he liked to joke the first few *T4* strands had been shot. Each week the crowds of screaming, cheering, heckling fans would swarm into the studios. And scream, cheer and heckle they did. That was part of the magic of the show. It was part of Dermot's job to both encourage it and control it. He would be walking a tightrope every week. And on live television there's no net to catch you if you fall.

'Everything is cool.' That's the calming, three-word message he was given from the producers. The auditions tapes were in the can. The back story recordings of the contestants' families and loved ones were ready to be played. The performers and the musicians were ready to give it their all. The only thing missing was Dermot to pull it all together.

The clock continued to tick. The 5pm start time drew ever closer. And then the final count began. 'Ladies and Gentlemen. It's *The X Factor*!' boomed out 'voice man' Peter Dickson as the crashing chords of the theme tune played. It was show time – and Dermot bounced out of the wings and across the stage to add the first greeting of his own.

'Good evening and welcome to *The X Factor*!'

On the page it's just a few short words. But in Dermot's mouth they had to come alive. All his life he has talked fast, sometimes too fast. But on television he wanted the pace to be infectious. He wanted it to tell viewers to hold on to their seats because they were in for a treat.

The first week's theme was Number One singles. But in a way the contestants' performances were overshadowed in the first live show. For Dermot had something very special to introduce – Leona Lewis was there to give her first live performance of 'Bleeding Love', the song that would take her to the top of the charts in the UK, the US and around the world. It made it quite a night.

'Thank you, goodbye, God bless and see you next week.' After Kimberley Southwick lost the judges' vote, and with that rush of words and one of his trademark salutes, Dermot signed off from the show. The credits rolled on television screens and the audience in London got to their feet – not to leave the studio but to carry on applauding. Dermot jumped up and down in a group hug with some of the production team – and let adrenaline carry him into his first set of post-show interviews with Fearne Cotton. It would be some time before he came down to earth.

'The first show was petrifying, absolutely petrifying, but in a really good way,' was his lovely way of describing the challenge. How did he get through it? 'I just thought: "I'll just try and enjoy it. I've rehearsed enough, live TV is what I do for a living, it's what I wanted to do as a boy and it's what I've done six nights a week for seven years on *BBLB* so I'll just enjoy it." But like I say, it was still petrifying. I know I drove everyone on the production team mad by constantly asking if everything was alright and then not believing them when they said it was,' he said. And early indications were that it had all been worth it. The show got 11 million viewers – 2.5 million more than the first episode of the third series the previous year. It was the highest figure for any *X Factor* opening show so far – not bad for a programme that many had said was at least a year past its sell-by date.

But how much of this success was down to Dermot, and how much was down to what television insiders called 'the Leona Lewis effect' – the realisation that stars really could be born on reality television? No one can really say. But for a while, at least Dermot's personal reviews were good. No surprise really that *Heat* magazine loved him – they knew full well that their readers adored Dermot. 'Dermot doing *The X Factor* has been a huge success. It's always incredibly entertaining but his just slightly barbed comments about some of the acts and the judges just makes the show slightly more credible than it used to be,' says *Heat*'s television editor Boyd Hilton.

Trouble was, the good news didn't last. And Dermot was as susceptible as anyone else to the old chestnut that one bad review can cancel out ten good ones and knock your confidence for six. First in the firing line were his clothes. 'Was a shiny suit really what Dermot should have been wearing at teatime on a Saturday afternoon?' asked one online critic. 'Ant and Dec look smart while staying relaxed. Dermot seemed to be making just a little too much of an effort. Clothes should make the man, not get in the way of him. Last night Dermot's clothes did just that. They were a distraction.' Some said he did seem too puppy dog, too eager to please – bouncing rather than striding across the stage. Others said his voice was too quick and his comments too muffled. 'The jury is still out on whether what works for youth television will go the distance in prime time.'

Most of the other commentary focused on how he compared to Kate Thornton, rather than simply judging his performance on its own merits. However high profile this role was, *The X Factor* wasn't a show he had originated himself. But he could make it his own. He would make a success out of *The X Factor*. Then he would have built the strongest foundations for his future.

In the meantime, Dermot did manage to laugh at one final set of criticism. The man who has always won female fans by sympathising with women who are judged so harshly on their appearance was about to suffer the same fate. His hair was the talk of the tabloids. In the run up to the live shows he had let it grow just that little bit longer than his traditional buzz cut. But had it worked? Some felt it was still too short for comfort. 'What is he trying to hide by keeping his hair so short? Does he really have tresses so wiry and ginger that to let them grow would make him look like a midget Ronald McDonald?' one newspaper columnist asked on the day of his second live show. Fortunately there was better news just around the corner. A new survey had been published in the *Radio Times*. The magazine had asked readers to list the ten 'coolest characters' on television. Dermot was at number seven, after a top three made up of Doctor Who, Jack Bauer from *24* and The Fonz from *Happy Days*. So number seven is good news? It is when a closer examination of the list reveals that of the top ten Dermot was the only one on the list who wasn't either fictional, a cartoon character or both!

The X Factor was rarely out of the headlines in the autumn of 2007 – and not always for the right reasons. Dermot had to deal with everything from threatened walk-outs from Sharon to the withdrawal of 15-year-old Emily after gang-related footage of her was spotted on the internet. But by the fourth week Dermot was well into the show's routine. He still arrived most Saturdays just after ten, he still worked on his scripts throughout the afternoon, and he got dolled up for the stage just after three. Between times he got used to having a constant stream of visitors coming in and out of his dressing room – competition winners often there wanting autographs and photographs, the directors needing a chat about the staging, and of course the camera crews from *The Xtra Factor* who had constant access to help them pad out the show.

Dermot had immediately bonded with Dannii because they were both newbies on the show and helped each other to find their feet in its first few weeks. But as time passed one question was starting to hit the press. Was there a hint of romance between these two beautiful people? *The X*

Factor's PR and publicity teams knew there was mileage in hinting about an on-set love affair. So hint they did. But in truth everyone knew that Dee had nothing to worry about. And anyway, in his characteristic, metrosexual fashion, eagle-eyed viewers said they thought Dermot flirted just as much with Simon as he did with Dannii. It was all part of the fresher, ever-so-slightly edgier approach Dermot brought to the show. It proved that he really could re-invigorate the brand.

What helped keep audiences on board – and made the show continue to beat the previous years' ratings – were the top-notch celebrity guests brought in to coach the contestants. Over the weeks, Dermot got to introduce everyone from Kylie Minogue and Michael Bublé to Westlife and Girls Aloud. And he had a fair few ups and downs along the way. The papers loved describing how superstar Céline Dion's contribution didn't exactly go as planned. 'The look of love turned into a look of anger' was how one of them put it when Dermot had to cut the diva off mid-sentence during her live show. When Dermot asked Céline how the contestants were all doing she had plenty to say. Too much, in fact. 'She really wouldn't stop and I had the producers in my ear telling me that if she carried on naming every single act on the show by telling us what she thought of them we would fall off the air before we got to the actual results. I had to shut her up and just had to say something. She has that very Québécois stare. Her management wasn't happy about it,' was how Dermot joked about it afterwards.

And in truth there was plenty to laugh about as the series gathered steam. Having worked so hard all summer Dermot loved being able to focus on just one main show. And this had been made a lot easier when his Radio Two bosses agreed to change the timeslot of his *Saturday Sessions* show and even consider some temporary, pre-recorded programmes to fit in with his new schedule. The fun was sometimes on display in front of the cameras – including when Dermot got carried away with the emotion and kissed Same Difference brother Sean along with his sister Sarah when the pair had faced another rough ride from the judges. Sometimes, though, the fun was off camera (or would have been if *The Xtra Factor* hadn't always been filming and insiders weren't breaking the rules by sometimes filming on mobile phones). One moment that made everyone laugh was when Dermot tried to sing along to 'Total Eclipse of the Heart' with contestant Niki Evans. Everyone on the show seemed to like Dermot's frequent presence during the rehearsals. They liked that he was a fully paid-up member of the show, not just a hired hand who turned up to read from a script and claim all the glory on a Saturday evening.

Dermot admits his job on the show was made a lot easier by the marvellous cast of characters who made it through to the final stages. In 2007 Rhydian Roberts was the ultimate 'Marmite man' that audiences either loved or hated. Dermot was in the first camp. He thought the 24-year-old Welshman was one of the strongest characters he had met – and a born crowd-pleaser. Dermot also took the younger man's side when he was mauled in the press, savagely attacked by Sharon, or mocked on the show for being accompanied by the music from *The Phantom of the Opera*.

Viewers seemed to like that Dermot always wore his heart on his sleeve.

When she had been hosting the show Kate had seemed to love absolutely everyone, so she seemed equally upset at each and every departure from the show. Dermot seemed to respect everyone equally. But watch closely and it seemed he liked some far more than others. When primary school teacher Beverly Trotman was voted off he seemed genuinely close to tears. When Same Difference faced down another deeply personal attack from the judges Dermot seemed to be affected almost as much as they were. It was touching stuff. And Dermot seemed to be growing more and more comfortable in his role.

The weeks flew by as the show raced towards its pre-Christmas finale. And it would end with a shock. Dermot stood back to let Rhydian and Leon Jackson soak up all the attention when all the viewers' votes had been counted. He looked down at the card in his hands one more time before calling out the name. It was always fun to spring a surprise. And this was a cracker.

'Leon!' One word and the madness began. The bookies lost a fortune that night, because everyone had been convinced that Rhydian had the show in the bag. The shock was such that the winning announcement was played on news broadcasts later that evening, Dermot's face was a picture as he hid the nation's shock and moved to congratulate and commiserate in equal measure. Swaying in the wings as Leon sang the series finale song 'When You Believe', Dermot was on an extraordinary high. The moment when a show ended was like nothing else on earth. All the worry, all the sleepless nights, all the adrenaline, and the excitement. All finally over – a tough job done well. The thrill saw Dermot through all the final interviews and photo shoots he did that final evening. He knew, of course, that the focus was now very firmly on Leon – and still, to some extent, on Rhydian. He could afford to play the avuncular uncle, smiling from the wings and wishing everyone well.

The live final had attracted the highest ratings in the four-year history of the show. It had beaten the moment in 2006 when Leona had been crowned a star.

One final piece of good news came through as Leon's first single headed to the top of the charts and gave the show its now customary Christmas Number One. Research showed that Dermot ended 2007 as the second most-watched television presenter in the country. Ant and Dec, of course, were the winners (they seemed joined at the hip as a single television entity), but Dermot was right on their toes. They had been seen by 51 per cent of the public at least once, according to the annual research by media agency MPG. Dermot, meanwhile, had been seen by 50 per cent of the public – making it a statistical dead heat. Ant, Dec and Dermot were well ahead of Phillip Schofield, then Gary Lineker in fourth place, and *Strictly Come Dancing*'s Tess Daly in fifth. Interestingly, Davina wasn't even in the top ten.

'Ant and Dec are the new Kings of British television presenting,' said MPG's strategy director Martyn Stokes when the annual research was unveiled. But it was clear that Dermot was the Crown Prince. And this was the man who two years earlier had worried he might get trapped for ever in a minority channel backwater or a cable channel hell. The third most watched man on British TV. Not bad for his debut year on *The X Factor*. Not bad in a year in which he had been too tired to be really creative on the show.

CHAPTER 17

NEW YEAR – NEW CHALLENGES

Dermot could have been excused for sleeping through Christmas 2007 because once 2008 was underway he had to be wide awake. He had a show to save. And he had a very big decision to make.

The show, of course, was *Celebrity Big Brother*. In January 2008 this was the new poisoned chalice of the broadcasting industry. A year before we had all watched aghast as the infamous 'racism' storm broke in the house. Shilpa Shetty, the ultimate winner of the series, had been the victim of the abuse and a media storm had engulfed model Danielle Lloyd, former pop star Jo O'Meara and Jade Goody, whose on-screen career it had all but ended. As that show had itself followed on the heels of the bullying and sheer nastiness of the previous year, when the show had included Pete Burns, Michael Barrymore and George Galloway, there had been plenty of calls for the whole *Celebrity Big Brother* concept to be dumped. It was also clear that very few big names wanted to be associated with the programme – either as contestants, presenters or commentators.

But after much soul searching among production company staff and Channel 4 executives the decision had been made to kick off 2008 with another series. This time Dermot, rather than Davina, would be the main host. And as usual he would multi-task – presenting *BBLB* alongside the main show.

His big decision was that he was going to quit the show after this one final outing. 'I thought I could have my cake and eat it,' he said of that mad schedule. And he was honourable enough to admit that he had been wrong. 'Both shows suffered as a result,' he accepted with refreshing honesty.

Of course, it would have been wonderful for Dermot's fans and for fans of *Big Brother*, if he had lasted out till the show's tenth anniversary, as it was rumoured that Davina intended to do. But by then Dermot would be 37 and critics could say that he was too old to be fronting a show full of teenagers. So for whatever reason – or whatever combination of reasons – Dermot dropped his bombshell in January 2008.

Endemol, Channel 4 and E4 bosses knew Dermot wasn't some drama queen angling for a pay rise or a higher profile. They knew how ragged he had been the previous summer and fully understood why he would want to avoid a repeat of a similar fate. So all the bosses could do was wish him well, thank him for his professionalism – and make it clear that there were no hard feelings. '*Big Brother's Little Brother* has been Dermot's Little Baby from the start. He was our first choice and the best choice. We will miss him and all the laughter and professionalism he has brought with him,' said Head of E4 Angela Jain. Everyone else on the series, from the boardroom to the studio floor, shared the sentiment. They vowed to make Dermot's final programmes the most memorable yet. If only they had known the show would end up making headlines for all the wrong reasons.

The plan for 2008 was to avoid any possibility of another set of celebrities behaving badly. So instead the house was to be filled with 'exceptional people' aged between 18 and 21, who had all been selected rather than auditioning for the show. The idea, so the producers said, was to pick interesting housemates who would have interesting life stories and interesting things to say.

But 'interesting' wasn't really why we all watch *Celebrity Big Brother*. We might not have approved of the antics of Barrymore, Burns, Galloway, Goody, Lloyd and so on. But we watched them and we talked about them for days. Without this kind of high-profile conflict would there be any point in tuning in? And how could the producers keep the word 'Celebrity' in the show's title when we hadn't heard of anyone in the house?

In the first week of January 2008 Dermot was one of only a small band of people who knew the answer. It was the concept of the celebrity hijack. The people in the house would be the 'interesting' unknowns. The people behind *Big Brother*'s microphone would be the celebrities. It was their turn to pull the strings. For a very brief period it looked as if the idea might pay off. When the *Big Brother: Celebrity Hijack* story broke it certainly made the news. Dermot was bombarded with questions about the format and – more importantly – about the identity of the celebrity hijackers. But Dermot couldn't say – not wouldn't, couldn't.

'I can honestly tell you that I haven't got a clue,' he said in January, as the clock ticked towards the show's launch. 'No one ever tells me, because I'm a terrible blabbermouth and hopeless about keeping secrets. If I know something I feel duty bound to tell the first person who asks. And that could be in an interview, in casual conversation, with friends, with friends of friends, loose acquaintances, with my newsagent, anyone.' What Dermot did know was that a lot was riding on the next few weeks. It might be his last spell in the *Big Brother* spotlight. But he felt he owed it to his colleagues to do a top job and keep the flame alive. If only he had known how tough this was going to be.

'Well, happy new year, *Big Brother* fans,' Dermot shouted above the noise from the crowd as the camera swirled around the gantries, the razor wire-topped walls and the sliding doors to the house itself. As usual, the audience was held back behind silver control barriers; there was a long walk from the cars, past the paparazzi and up to the entrance to the house. As usual, everyone was desperate to find out who would be in their sights. And the word 'Who?' turned out to be particularly appropriate. It turned out that a fair few fans hadn't believed the pre-publicity about the celebrity-free *Celebrity Big Brother* series. Many had thought that it must be a joke and that the usual gallery of grotesques, wannabes and never-beens would soon be parading in front of them.

The atmosphere wasn't great as the penny dropped. One

by one the housemates were all introduced with their mini videos and walked the walk to the house door. Dermot had to try and keep the enthusiasm high. It wasn't easy. And this was only the start. As we got to know the first housemate, young Scottish political hopeful John Loughton, Dermot moved on to stage two. He had a handshake and a hug for first celebrity hijacker, Matt Lucas in the 'hijack booth'. And he had a lot of explaining to do. The concept for the show wasn't simple. It was hard to see whether it would be worth watching. And while it made good television, it wasn't easy for Dermot to get the message across while Matt hammed it up and pulled faces just behind him.

'It was all a bit of a mess,' was one of the kindest comments posted on the net that night as fans digested the new world order. That proved to be one of the better responses to Dermot's big night. The following day the only thing the critics had liked had been Dermot's 'gorgeous' toffee-coloured pea coat and black leather gloves. Fashion aside, hardly anyone had a good word for the show.

'Bored, bored, bored,' said on viewer in another online chatroom. 'Too embarrassing to watch,' wrote another. 'What's happened to *Big Brother*? Davina is best out of this and why Dermot O'Leary put his name to this is beyond me,' concluded a third. But Dermot had tried to work the crowds and work some magic.

As well as his much-loved coat, Dermot had been wearing a black scarf, black gloves and jeans as he had walked and talked across the set -- and into the production offices. He certainly had the kind of style and pace that Davina had made her own. And he thought he had something else to offer. The producers wanted him to show off more of the behind-the-scenes world of the show – just as he had done all those years earlier on the first ever *BBLB*. But wasn't that the problem? Hadn't we all seen the banks of monitors before? 'This is brilliant and it can only get brillianter!' Dermot screeched at one point as the housemates made their tense, nervous introductions. But in truth it wasn't brilliant at all.

'I love it. We're on a roll,' he said. But that was wrong too.

Dermot's big night got less than half the audience of *Celebrity Big Brother* 2007 – a peak of 3.5 million compared to that show's 7.3 million. 'Don't go away. See you in a tick,' Dermot said as his second commercial break arrived – his relaxed, cheeky persona intact. But people did go away. In their millions.

By the end of the first show a catastrophic two million of Dermot's early audience failed to follow him over to E4 for the rest of the night's coverage. And when the evening ended the figures showed it had been a resounding flop. None of the four previous *Celebrity Big Brother* preview shows had attracted less than 4.4 million. Dermot's average over the course of the vital first night had been far less than half this total. And it wasn't as if rival channels had brought out any big shows to try and steal viewers. They were treating it as an ordinary night with repeated comedy shows on BBC Two and no great excitement anywhere else. It seemed that in the broadcasting world no one felt threatened by Dermot's latest venture. They were right to be so relaxed. By the time Dermot got to day four, in television terms he was as good as talking to himself – some of his ratings were so low as to be close to being statistically irrelevant.

Embarrassing? Yes it was. Humiliating? Just a little – especially when the reviews came in. 'Let's start the year on a positive note and congratulate Davina McCall,' wrote Ian Hyland in the *News of the World*. 'Avoiding this calamity has to be the first great decision of her career. And that makes you feel even worse for Dermot. He's been waiting in the wings for so long he hasn't noticed he's gotten old. And now, with housemates young enough to be his kids, he's facing exactly the same challenge Davina has been tackling since *Big Brother 3*: pretending to enjoy something when your heart is not in it.'

That hurt, Dermot was forced to admit. And it wasn't all.

'Could anyone save a dire sinking ship like this *Celebrity Big Brother*?' asked columnist Sebastian Barker in *thelondonpaper*. 'Maybe a very clever presenter could have done so. Maybe a presenter who sends it up the way Terry Wogan sends up Eurovision. What's clear is that Dermot is no Terry Wogan. He treated the show with reverence and seriousness when it deserved neither. It needed someone to pick through it and expose it for the joke it was. Then we might have been able to laugh at it all. Jonathan Ross or Russell Brand may have been able to bring the right tone to the task. Dermot didn't. He made the mistake of doing what his bosses wanted rather that what us viewers wanted. If he had found the courage of his convictions and said, yes, it's all a bit dreadful this year then the show might have worked. Telling us how great it was just didn't work. The show won't kill O'Leary's career but for a while it will probably stop him earning any decent money from commercials. After his wild claims about how wonderful *Celebrity Big Brother* was going to be no one will ever believe a word he says again.'

However much the review stung, Dermot couldn't just hide away to lick his wounds. *Big Brother: Celebrity Hijack* was a full-on, 24/7 production. Dermot was due back on set, day after day, faking ever more enthusiasm and feeling ever more desperate.

Worse still, he had to invite Russell on to the set as a celebrity hijacker (he was one of the most exciting to watch) alongside other big names such as Joan Rivers, Ian Wright and Roseanne Barr. Was it the final humiliation that Russell's show was one of the most fun moments of the entire series?

As the days passed the show pretty much disappeared without trace. Its ratings fell off the cliff, none of the papers or celebrity magazines were even the slightest bit interested in the housemates. So by the time that John Loughton, the first housemate to hit the screen on day one, was named the show's winner and collected his £50,000 prize it was clear that nobody cared. The tabloids pretty much ignored the coronation.

'It's Day 26 and after 7 years and 511 editions of *Big Brother's Little Brother* Dermot O'Leary is very nearly at the end of his last ever show. Only one thing remains. Dermot – here are your Best Bits.' That oh-so-familiar voice of Marcus Bentley was played in the *BBLB* studio as Dermot sat on the sofa for the very last time. Up next was a fantastic set of clips – all the mad-cap moments, stupid costumes, bloopers, highs and lows that Dermot had given us since 2001. It's fair to say that those compiling the Best Bits hadn't been short of material. 'All the best from *BBLB*' was the final message on the screen as the compilation faded to black at the end.

'It's been the best seven years of my life,' Dermot said as the credits began to fly along the base of the *BBLB* screen. Eagle-eyed viewers reckoned they could see a tear in his eye as he flashed a look beyond the cameras at the crew. And as he spoke to the press afterwards he made it clear how much he would miss the show. '*Big Brother* has been the defining show of my career,' he said. And yes, he was fiercely proud of it. 'It's a show that started out in a little broom cupboard and grew to be a daily show on Channel 4 and has a cult following that has stayed with it. I'm very, very proud of it and I will miss it a great deal. It's also been an extraordinary apprenticeship for any other show I may choose to do.'

The final comment just sort of slipped out. In truth Dermot had no intention of doing any other show for quite some time. Nor did he need to. Yes, *Celebrity Hijack* had been a bit of a disaster, but did that really matter in the grand scheme of things? The simple fact was that Dermot's final *Big Brother* commitment was over. Everyone had known in advance that this was his final series, so no-one could accuse him of being like some kind of opportunistic rat leaving a sinking ship. Another presenter could take up the *Big Brother* baton in the future. Dermot was ready to move on.

CHAPTER 18

PRESENTING DERMOT O'LEARY

If the past ten years had all about building up Dermot O'Leary the television professional, then the spring and summer of 2008 would be all about consolidating Dermot O'Leary the man. Anyone who wants to know what he is capable of on screen or on air needs to look back to his body of work since Xfm and *T4*. Anyone who wants to know what he is truly like needs only look at what he chose to do from the end of *Celebrity Big Brother* onwards. That's when a free diary finally allowed him to reconsider his true priorities.

No surprise that when freedom finally hit his two first ports of call were sport and family. He caught a few late season Arsenal games at the Emirates stadium and spent a few long weekends with his family in Essex – for once not worrying too much if he had an extra pint of Guinness down the pub. He and Dee also hopped over to visit her family in Norway.

One of Dermot's great pieces of good fortune is that his

lifestyle has never really matched his earnings. Not for him a fancy mansion in a posh postcode or a string of holiday homes in the sun. On a smaller scale, his disinterest in the celebrity world meant that he and Dee didn't spend vast amounts of cash in fancy restaurants or nightclubs. They paid for seats at the front of the plane when they travelled. But in most other ways they bucked the 'spend spend spend' trends of the nation. Turning convention on its head and living a 'lemonade lifestyle on champagne money' meant they had plenty of money in the bank – a very hefty cushion against bad times in the future. For a workaholic like Dermot, who has had part-time jobs since his early teens, this was important. But it certainly didn't make him complacent. His spiritual side told him that if his own needs were met, then it was time to pay attention to those less fortunate than himself.

So, with time on his hands at last, Dermot dusted down his list of favourite charities and got to work.

Over the years charity insiders say Dermot has been one of the lowest-profile but most diligent fund- and awareness-raisers around. Not for him the high profile but largely meaningless role as a UN Goodwill Ambassador or figurehead patron. Instead he does things the old-fashioned way, finding causes he believes in and rolling up his sleeves to help.

Ever since his student days at Middlesex University Dermot has followed the tortured wranglings over Third World debts. He was a big and an early supporter of the Make Poverty History campaign as the old socialist in him couldn't accept the huge gulf between rich and poor nations, or the lottery that guarantees those born in one place a longer, healthier and more peaceful life than those born elsewhere. Over the years Dermot's involvement with this issue has deepened. By 2005 he had met with many of the top brass in the debt charity world – and at one point he discussed new ways to develop debt relief at a focus group attended by none other than Tony Blair, Gordon Brown and Bill Clinton.

A less fashionable charity Dermot has supported for years is Cafod, the Catholic Agency For Overseas Development that works to provide emergency relief and long-term development help in developing countries and trouble spots around the world. Once more Dermot was determined to be more than just a figurehead. And if he was going to write a lot of big cheques he wanted to know exactly where his money was going. That's why, in 2004, Dermot and his dad had agreed to visit war-torn Sierra Leone to see first hand the challenges the aid workers faced – and the solutions they could provide. The trip was tough and the pair saw some harrowing sights on the road. And back at home Dermot felt even more conflict about his own good fortune. So he and Sean decided to redouble their fund-raising efforts. They talked long into the night. And then they finally agreed to sign up for a charity version of *Who Wants To Be A Millionaire?* The decision to appear was a tough one because Dermot had successfully guarded his family's privacy for so long. Could he now be opening them up to unwelcome attention?

Dermot knew full well that once the media genie is out of the bottle then it's out for good. The papers didn't respond well to people who demanded privacy one day then appeared all over television or the magazines the next. Sure, *Millionaire* was for charity. But it could still blow the O'Leary family's delicate balance right out of the water.

But in the end the *Millionaire* magic couldn't be denied. Most of the other celebrities who go on the charity shows say the same: there simply isn't any other way you can raise so much money, so quickly – and tell several million people about your favourite cause at the same time. Chris Tarrant always gives each contestant a few moments to describe the charity they want to help – and they normally get to repeat or add to the message later in the show if they last long enough. Charities say it is an invaluable piece of publicity – raising awareness as well as funds. After seeing such horrors in Sierra Leone, Dermot and Sean knew they couldn't deny either to Cafod. So off they went to sit on those famous high stools and aim for the million-pound jackpot.

In the Green Room, where performers wait before going on stage and on camera, dad and son were both feeling the heat. Sean, not surprisingly, was bothered by the simple fact of being on national television. Dermot was well aware that he was stepping a long way from his normal comfort zone – and that if he did badly it would be a huge missed opportunity for Cafod.

'OK, we're ready to go. Do you want to follow me, please?'

Dermot smiled as the typically black-clad researcher led him and his dad to the shiny *Millionaire* set. How often had his own researchers led even more nervous guests to the studio? How had he managed to avoid giving televised interviews himself for so long?

The crashing chords of the *Who Wants To Be A Millionaire?* theme tune heralded their arrival, Chris gave his usual welcome, the cash race was on and Dermot was first to score a win. He got the first 'joke' question right – 'What phrase is used to describe words that are written without the use of capital letters?' (It was, of course Lower Case, rather than Lower Rucksack, Lower Bag or Lower Holdall.) From then on Sean pretty much took charge – answering most questions until the pair were on the point of reaching the £132,000 level. Both men knew exactly how much good this much cash could do around the world. And surely they were the right team to win it – because of all things the next question had a rare religious flavour. Get it right and the money got even bigger. Get it wrong and the pair's payout would fall to just £32,000. So, which Bishop wasn't automatically a member of the House of Lords?

'Are you sure you want to play?' Chris asked, very aware of the tight-rope walk his guests had embarked upon. Dad and son looked at each other and decided to go for it. And they got it wrong (it's the Bishop of Salisbury, not the Bishop of London). The O'Learys were gutted, though they did find one small way to soften the blow for Cafod. To Dermot's surprise the *Who Wants to be a Millionaire?* producers pay the celebrity contestants a £500 fee for doing the charity show. By adding this to their pot Dermot and Sean were able to give Cafod a slightly higher £33,000.

Dermot's next charity challenge was to get his running shoes back on and hit the streets. Over the years he has continued to do as many marathons and half-marathons as his work schedule will allow. And the smiling, laid back man from the telly becomes fiercely competitive when the chips are down. When he was raising more funds for Cafod by doing the 13-mile Great North Run just after *Millionaire*, he was only able to record a personal best on a 'hellish' day because he didn't want to be beaten by a couple of runners dressed as beefburgers and an incredibly fit 60-year-old fellow runner he called 'Ken the Gazelle'.

Down in London the following year Dermot was happy to raise eyebrows in his next fund-raising effort. He wore 'possibly the loudest vest in the world' in support of the HIV and Aids charity the Terrence Higgins Trust. 'Dermot's getting hot and sweaty for the THT' was his fund-raising slogan. It worked. He beat his original target by some 50 per cent. Other charities have also benefited from Dermot's unwillingness to take himself too seriously – and his understanding that sex can sell. Just after Gareth Gates had made the finals of *Pop Idol* the white suit he had worn on the show came up at an auction Dermot was hosting for a different HIV charity, Crusaid. Dermot joked to his well-heeled audience that if the suit fitted him he would bid for it himself. Then he got his kit off on stage (well, he stripped down to his boxer shorts) to try and answer his own question and bring the *Heat*-sponsored auction alive. Funnily enough, despite getting the rapt attention of most of the women (and a fair few men) in the audience, Dermot ended up with the winning bid on the suit. He spent £15,000 on it – though away from the excitement of the auction stage Dermot soon realised that it was, indeed, too tight for him to wear.

Centrepoint, the charity that helps young, homeless people in London and across the country is another cause Dermot tries hard to support. But much closer to his heart is something else: cancer research, relief and care.

Dermot has personally known people touched by the disease. That's why he has always gone the extra mile for the charities that came through when those he loved needed them the most.

He became a patron of the Everyman charity as far back as March 2002. Everyman is part of the Institute of Cancer Research and its backers say Dermot is the perfect person to front its campaigns. Medical experts say men are particularly hard to reach in most prevention and early intervention campaigns – an unwillingness to admit to vulnerability forcing most to suffer in silence. But if Dermot was ready to deal with something like testicular cancer, everyone could be unembarrassed about dealing with it. It was a perfect message – and Dermot was always ready to join in the fun to help point it out. He's been in the ground-breaking 'big balls' campaigns. And he has even broken one of his key self-imposed rules to help raise awareness of cancer issues. Ever since hitting the screen as a beefy-armed newcomer on *T4* all those years ago Dermot has been offered big money for sexy photo shoots. In 2001, for example, he was presented with a particularly large deal for a racy Dermot O'Leary calendar. But he always said no. Until the Institute of Cancer Research asked the question. It was putting together a series of snaps for its Everyman campaign.

And knowing what he did about the disease Dermot knew he couldn't turn them down.

By 2008 Dermot is estimated to have raised well over £100,000 for his key charities – excluding the *Millionaire* cash. He has also raised the profile of several vital health care messages. Nothing is certain. But one thing is a pretty sure bet: Dermot's good works will continue.

After *Big Brother: Celebrity Hijack* ended Dermot had one more surprise for some of his fans. He was going to talk about religion again. In January 2008 he knew, no one knew better, that British public figures who profess their faith are often ridiculed. He knew, therefore, that the easy option was to keep those thoughts quiet. So when Cafod asked him to support the year's Family Fast Day in Lent he could have taken the 'expert' advice and turned it down. But Dermot said yes. And in the process he won a lot of friends – of all faiths and none.

'Do I worry about how it will impact upon my image?' he said when he was asked about the new role. His answer could hardly be faulted. 'Well, for me, your image is only as honest as you are. As an actor or a pop star there is a veneer. But when you are a presenter there's just you. It might be you as you would be at a party, making sure that everyone is having a good time, rather than you at home having dinner with your family. But it's still you. Your image is still a side of you. And my Catholicism is part of me,' he told *Daily Telegraph* reporter Peter Stanford. Dermot went on to talk about an old interview he had recently read of the late Brian Clough. 'It was to do with socialism and success. He said:

"Why are the two seen as mutually exclusive? If I'm doing well, it doesn't make me any less of a socialist if I have a bottle of Champagne." And I thought that is so true. The same can be said of combining your religious beliefs with working on Saturday night TV. I don't believe that anyone should be defined or judged by their faith. So when people watch me on a Saturday night they shouldn't think of me as any different from anyone else.'

But even by saying these words, and expressing these carefully thought-out opinions, Dermot was proving he was different from others. He was proving that he had intelligence and integrity. 'I'm not interested in preaching from the rooftops,' was how he rounded out this most tricky of subjects. 'All I do is show in public my own faith. I was brought up with it, and I still practise, but I don't think that my God is any more worthy than that of a friend of mine, who happens to follow Allah.'

What Dermot could have done in early 2008 was cash in on his elevation to the prime-time elite. He could have gone for even bigger fame – and bigger bucks – with a show in America. Over the past few years a surprising number of very British presenters have followed the likes of Simon Cowell and Anne Robinson and made a fortune on network television stateside. Tim Vincent now fronts up *Access Hollywood*; Denise Van Outen was a judge on NBC's *Grease: You're The One That I Want*, Cat Deeley had a role on *American Idol*, and there were plenty of British judges on everything from *America's Got Talent* to *Dancing With The Stars*. And if comedy actors like Hugh Laurie can head up shows like *House* and former soap stars like Michelle Ryan can play the lead in *The Bionic Woman* then surely Dermot could find a niche of his own in the Californian sunshine?

Over the years he has certainly had some interesting offers – which increased after he met the *American Idol* producers in early 2007. But once more Dermot was 'Dr No'. One reason for the refusal is that he has conflicting thoughts about the States. On the one hand he loves it – especially New York, which has a special place in most Irish hearts. And the latent ambition that has driven him so far does keep telling him to go west for more of the same. But his love of privacy always holds him back. He loves being able to disappear into a crowd when he is in America. He loves just being another anonymous Brit when he meets people there. And in many ways he thinks this anonymity is what keeps his feet so firmly on the ground. Whenever people call him a sex symbol he makes the point that he only turns heads in the UK – which must mean it is only his fame that people notice. 'I've just been in America and women didn't look at me twice,' the *Independent* reported him as saying in 2007.

As was revealed in the *Independent* in September 2007, Dermot's 'one indulgence' remains the ability to turn left and head for business or first-class cabins when he flies. He is also flexible in his travel. When he was coming back from a ski trip in St Anton, according to the same article, deep snow meant long delays in his budget flight.

After being sent back to the terminal the passengers were told they should all go away and come back tomorrow. 'But not only would the airline not guarantee when we would leaving they couldn't give us our luggage back either,' Dermot said. Up for a challenge Dermot instead took a train to Strasbourg then to Paris where he jumped on the Eurostar to get him back to London. It wasn't cheap but it beat the plane and made him wary of budget airlines ever since, he said.

As well as ski trips, he admits he is 'seduced' by Italy and loves the south-west coast of France and the faded glory of places like Biarritz. He also admits to being 'a water-baby' so after a few days of doing nothing he wants to go swimming, diving or surfing rather than stay put on a beach. Sometimes October finds him in Cornwall, surfing in water he says is far warmer than you might imagine. And many weekends a year he visits his parents in Colchester, often having days out across the border in Suffolk at places like Aldeburgh.

So could his fascination with travel give him a new career option in 2008 and beyond? Many people wonder why Dermot hasn't yet followed in another pair of sexy Irish footsteps and become the new Craig Doyle with a travel show. Ask him his favourite places in the world, as the *Independent* did, and he can name hotels in South Africa (The Lodge on the Bay in Plettenberg on the Garden Route out of Cape Town), favourite drives (Route E6 in Norway, which has mountains on one side and fjords on the other), and his favourite meal (at The Boiling Pot in Austin, Texas where you can get everything from lobster to potatoes and frankfurters all in the same meal). On his 'must visit someday soon' list are Russia and South America, and he wants the time for some long walking holidays in places like Montana, Vermont and Maine. And don't forget the UK – he reckons we sell ourselves short by always wanting to holiday overseas. 'It is still a green and pleasant land,' he told the *Independent*'s readers.

Dermot's big surprise in 2008 was that opting out of *Big Brother* hadn't limited his career options. The fact that people knew he was more available seemed to be adding to them. But he is the first to admit that some of the offers were never going to fly.

One was for the role of Billy Flynn in the stage musical *Chicago* – where he could have performed alongside former *X Factor* contestant Brenda Edwards. He had to turn the opportunity down. He reckoned his 'one note' singing voice was fine for Irish christenings and funerals but not that great for anything else. Or was it? Another offer came in for a spot on *Celebrity Stars in Their Eyes*. For a moment Dermot was tempted to say yes – he says he knows the show is cheesy and silly, but he's always had a secret dream of taking part. His agent, however, was less keen. 'He said: "I beg you not to do this show". He knew I'd make a tit of myself,' Dermot admits. So that too is a professional dream Dermot is still to realise.

More seriously, he did spend the first half of 2008 dusting down other career ambitions. And they suggest that in the long term, hosting *X Factor* won't be enough for him.

Dermot has recently said a new name has cropped up on his list of all-time telly heroes. It's not a light-entertainment star like Terry Wogan, Jonathan Ross or Chris Evans. It's the much more highbrow David Dimbleby. In 2005 Dermot had loved the BBC's *A Picture of Britain* in which David had explored British and Irish history through art. Two years later he had also loved the architectural follow up, *How We Built Britain*. So was that the sort of show Dermot really wanted to make? Absolutely. 'That kind of thing is my ultimate goal. David Dimbleby is just immense.'

His other ambition is more long term. He wants to be a prime-time chat show host by the time he hits 40 – in 2013. It's a dream he has had since his Essex childhood, when he, his mum and sister would all sit down to watch *Wogan* three times a week. Unknown to most people outside the broadcasting world, he had seriously considered an offer of a chat show back in 2004 when he was working on *Shattered*. But had quite rightly guessed that the timing was all wrong. 'There's a glut of those kinds of shows so I'd be slaughtered,' he told pals. 'There's no point in doing a talk show if you're just getting the guests that Ross and Parkinson have turned down.' That's what happened to Johnny Vaughan when he tried to muscle in on the old-timers' territory that year. 'Johnny's a great presenter but if you come over from Hollywood and you've got the chance to go on a show that's watched by 7 million or a show on BBC Three you're going to go for the 7 million,' Dermot said. So he decided to play a waiting game. He thought back to 1989 when he had seen his hero Jonathan Ross crash and burn with his much hyped but ill-fated series *One Hour with Jonathan Ross*. That same year he had seen comedian Ben Elton look uncomfortable when he took over the host's chair on *Wogan* during Terry's summer break. In the years ahead he would see Davina McCall, Lily Allen, Charlotte Church and a host of others all fail because they signed up for the wrong format at the wrong time.

By 2008 he was still biding his time. And he did finally feel ready for the task. For a while television insiders had been dubious about Dermot's ability to command the talk show market. Of the great chat show hosts they said Terry Wogan had a surprising darkness underlying his Irish geniality. Michael Parkinson had the life experience to know when to come up with the difficult question and Jonathan Ross has the extraordinary, lightening fast zest and racy mind that suited his market. All three brought some complexity to the chat show party. And until recently Dermot has been seen as too open, too eager to please. 'Depth will come with age. I'm still learning,' he had said at 32, when he'd first given himself that 'chat show by 40' deadline. Today he feels he is closer to the goal than ever.

And this wasn't his only professional passion. *The X Factor* had given him a taste for mainstream television. But in his heart of hearts could there have been a worry that he didn't entirely own the show? Could he have thought that having taken over from Kate Thornton, were there some people who would always see him in her shadow?

From now on this wasn't going to be enough for Dermot. And he was no longer shy of saying so. He no longer felt any need to keep his ambition under wraps. 'I do want to create the next big live television show. Like *TFI Friday* or *The Big Breakfast*. I want to be remembered as a TV institution. Until I get a show that I drive I can't consider myself a major presenter,' he said.

As spring turned to summer in 2008 Dermot and Dee were

planning to spend even more quality time together. 'It's my first summer in seven years,' Dermot said, having seen all of the previous ones swallowed up by his workload on *BBLB*. And as he waited to see who – if anyone – would be drafted in to replace him on the show for 2008 he admitted that he probably wouldn't be able to watch it.

'There won't be any resentment because it was my decision to move on. But I will be jealous,' he said. And he knew he would miss the 'back from the holidays' atmosphere when so many of the same crew always came back together for the latest series. Now he had graduated from that close knit gang. It would take a while to accept that they would now be having fun, and building memories, with someone new. The endless web-searching, tabloid-reading and lateral thinking that had always been required to keep ahead of the keenest *BBLB* fans was demanding but all part of the process of making television programmes.

So did Dermot and Dee have anything else to tell us all now that their lives were on a more even keel? Could wedding bells, and children, finally be around the corner?

Having started dating seven years ago Dermot and Dee had taken their time before moving in together. And even then Dermot admits he hadn't quite been prepared for the change of lifestyle this would entail. 'I'm watching a lot less sport,' he told the Female First website soon after Dee moved in, in the early spring of 2005. 'I have to negotiate how much live sport I can see. Dee always says: "Can't you tape it?" And I'm: "Of course not! It's live sport. It doesn't work like that," which she doesn't quite get.' Arsenal games were allowed, though, and in truth Dermot was thrilled to have his girlfriend so close.

Fast forward to 2008 and nothing had changed. Though Dermot, ever the gentleman, was still very conscious of his girlfriend's feelings. 'I think our relationship would have to go catastrophically wrong not to get married at some time,' he said. 'I love my girlfriend and she loves me. One day I hope we'll get married. But she's five years younger than me and, whether you like it or not, marriage can't help but put slight constraints on a relationship because you've got more responsibility. I don't want Dee thinking that she can't further her career because she's got a band of gold on her finger.'

It was a brave, well-thought-out statement. And it was the same when anyone brought up the subject of children. Dermot claims he has never been obsessively paternal or broody (though he kissed Davina's bump before every *Big Brother* show when she was pregnant and spends a lot of time with his mates' kids). So he reckons he and Dee will start a family 'when the time is right. I'm with the person I want to be with and that's fine for now,' are his final words on the subject. As usual he pulls the shutters down fast when talk gets too personal.

The *X-Factor* treadmill was a lot easier to ride from 2008 onwards with *BBLB* out of the way. But Dermot certainly didn't seem to have any extra free time. Job offers continued to flood in. And in 2009 one of them gave Dermot a taste of global, internet fame: by making him the last man alive to introduce Michael Jackson to the world's media.

'This is it,' Michael had said when he announced his

unprecedented residency at London's O2 arena. And that was it, as the world found out, to its horror, less than four months later when the star was found dead in his Californian home. To date more than 2 million people have watched all the various internet clips of Michael hugging Dermot as he took to the stage. Amidst chaotic scenes, and with the words: 'London welcomes the King of Pop: Michael Jackson,' Dermot had made it to the centre of the biggest show-business story of the decade. And while he did joke about the occasion to *Soccer AM* when Michael was still alive, he never went on to repeat any of the stories after his death. Instead Dermot refused to join the rent-a-quote crowd and offer any opinions on Michael's health or state of mind. He chose to remain discreet, honest and loyal. He acted like a gentleman.

Funnily enough those same gentlemanly instincts came to the fore several other times in the second half of 2009. How about the time one of the straps on Whitney Houston's dress appeared to snap while she sang on the *X-Factor*? Should Dermot leap forward to help? Stand back and pretend no-one had noticed? Or carry on with the show regardless? He did the latter – just as he did amidst all the audience confusion when Janet Jackson sang on the show but wasn't asked any of the usual 'what do you think about the contestants?' questions afterwards. With Dannii Minogue giving birth to her first baby, Cheryl Cole contracting malaria and Louis Walsh hitting the headlines by commenting on all the various replacement judges there was no shortage of *X-Factor* upheavals in 2010. Dermot, though, sailed through them all. The producers could hardly fail to notice how useful it was to have such a strong man amidst the madness. So how might they reward him?

Rumours that he would host the show if and when it launched in America – possibly even in Las Vegas – came thick and fast throughout the summer of 2010. There was certainly a lot of precedent for the idea. Cat Deeley had recently become the latest in a long line of British presenters to take over big US shows. A clean-cut Irishman like Dermot would surely go down a storm in America. So would Dermot take the job if it was offered?

In some ways the question takes him back full circle to 2007 when he took over Britain's *X-Factor* from Kate Thornton. The fear then was that too much fame could destroy the privacy he craved. 'I have never walked down the street noting how many people recognise me,' he said once. 'All I have ever wanted is to do my job as well as I can, for as long as I can.' In many ways the fact that his job involved cameras, microphones and audiences was incidental. And that, perhaps, is the real reason why TV insiders say Dermot has achieved the impossible: he has become hugely famous, yet has never let fame change him. He has become rich, yet has never let the money change him either. Even before a possible move to America he has hit the entertainment heights while keeping his feet firmly planted on the floor. That's a pretty tough trick to master. It's not something he's likely to change any time soon.

'I've always known all this could end at any time,' he said once. But as the years pass the likelihood of this happening faces almost to zero. In a world of instant fame Dermot has proved himself to be the real deal. He has worked at his craft.

He has found out exactly what works, and what doesn't. And he has never had to compromise or pretend to be anything that he's not. Whether he is in Highbury or Hollywood the outsider from Essex is still far more likely to be found in an ordinary pub or bar than at a glitzy show-business party. He's more likely to be at an old friend's house than at a high profile awards ceremony. That's how he lives his life. That's how he sees his future. And that, ultimately, is his 'X-factor'.